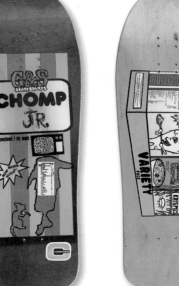

THE SKATEBOARD

THE GOOD

THE RAD

AND THE GNARLY

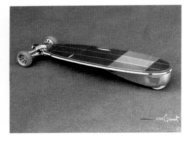

There are no official records documenting the progress of skateboarding in the reference sections of your local libraries . . . there's no "official" version of skateboarding, no one has any claims to ownership.

Moments in Time, from *Sidewalk Surfer,* No. 12, December 1996

The author, circa 1970, styling on a Hobie Super Surfer with composition wheels in sunny Santa Cruz, California. Photo by Mom.

The innovation of urethane wheels in the early 1970s was like the starter's gun for the Oklahoma Land Rush of 1889. Anything was possible with plastics, and the race was on for pipes, pools, and parks. *George Rose/Getty Images*

from the Lipton Tea factory. Somehow that photo ended up on the back cover of one of the first skateboard books of the urethane era, *Anybody's Skateboard Book*.

I graduated from high school in 1978, and that's pretty much where skateboarding ended for me and a lot of my friends. As I researched this book and talked to other skateboarders, that seemed to be the pattern. You start skateboarding as a kid, get really into it as a teenager, have a blast with your friends through high school, and then all that enthusiasm is dispersed after graduation—by college, commitments, age.

My skateboard cred starts to fade after the 1970s, even though I worked at *Surfer* magazine for ten years, most of that with Steve Hawk, brother of Tony. At some point in the early 1990s, I visited Tony's house in Fallbrook, California, where he had an epic backyard ramp set up. It was then that I witnessed firsthand how far skateboarding had come.

I've written nine books on various aspects of surfing, but this book is by far the most difficult and time-consuming book I have ever done. I knew I was in trouble when I walked into Larry Balma's barn in east Oceanside and saw the hundreds of skateboard magazines and industry journals he'd collected and carefully saved over the years. If I sat there for four years I don't think I'd be able to read it all.

But I pushed on, piecing this book together from books, videos, and online articles, and interviews with dozens of people, from 1940s skater Carl Knox to the Sector 9 guys at an ASR show. Of all the resources I used for this book, two of the best for IDing skateboards were the *Disposable* books by Sean Cliver and www.artofskateboarding.com.

All told, there were probably twenty thousand distinct skateboard decks that have been made since the late 1950s. This book isn't meant to identify the provenance of every deck, wheel, truck, and accessory ever made, but to detail the "arc" of skateboarding—if I can use a Hollywood term—and highlight the most important people, events, boards, and innovations to show how skateboarding, begun as a crude sport invented by surfers in the late 1940s, became a multi-billion dollar industry and sport practiced by millions around the world.

Perhaps even more importantly, this book celebrates all that simple fun my friends and I had skateboarding.

Ben Marcus
Malibu, California

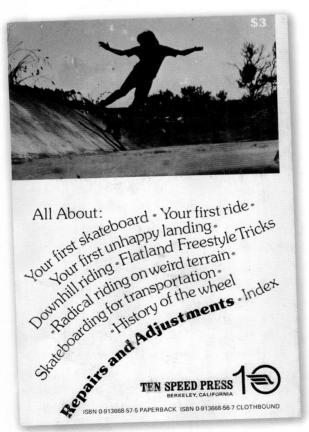

All About:
Your first skateboard • Your first ride •
Your first unhappy landing •
Downhill riding • Flatland Freestyle Tricks
Radical riding on weird terrain •
Skateboarding for transportation •
• History of the wheel
Repairs and Adjustments • Index

TEN SPEED PRESS 10
BERKELEY, CALIFORNIA

ISBN 0-913668-57-5 PAPERBACK   ISBN 0-913668-56-7 CLOTHBOUND

The author, skateboarding on Cadillac wheels at Liptons, on the west side of Santa Cruz. This photo appeared on the back cover of *Anybody's Skateboard Book*. Kevin Reed

Young devils on the loose and having too much fun: a cabal of kids on orange-crate scooters tear up a street in central Boston, circa 1955.
Three Lions/Getty Images

them shorter, lighter, faster, and more fun. California had a bigger surf scene in 1947 then most people realize, so it makes sense that the skateboard was born around this time.

The genesis of skateboarding might have been as simple as this: Surfing kids in the 1940s were lugging around hardwood surfboards made of redwood and balsa, which were lighter than previous boards, but still heavy. Kids wanted to get those boards to the beach and they needed two hands. A bicycle was no good, and neither was a scooter. So they kicked the orange

Continued on page 32

Fifties skateboard technology: metal roller-skate wheels and trucks nailed— not even screwed—to a piece of 2x4. It's a wonder anyone survived.
Courtesy G&S

A crude 1950s homemade cruiser. This board shows there was some experimentation at the time: where most kids were content to nail roller-skate wheels to a 2x4, other high-tech kids actually used screws, and many went wider, using a 1x6. Structural advantages of the 1x6 over the 2x4 are unknown. *Courtesy G&S*

There was some design variation in roller-skating wheels and trucks, which were adapted to early skateboards in the 1950s. Functional advantages unknown. Kids just used what they could beg, borrow, or steal.
Courtesy Rich Novak/Santa Cruz Skateboards

Surfing went from chic to ever-so cooler. A Hawaiian surfing lass in the 1930s. Miklos "Miki" Dora and friend, having fun in the sun and sand, in the 1960s.

RIDING GIANTS

MIKE DOYLE WONDERS HOW THEY SURVIVED

Mike Doyle was "arguably the 1960s's all-around best surfer" according to Matt Warshaw's *Encyclopedia of Surfing*. A surfer, tandem surfer, paddler, and all-around waterman, Doyle was born in Los Angeles in 1941 and started surfing in 1954 at Manhattan Beach. He went on to become one of the founders of the surf industrial complex, involved with Surf Research, the Single Ski, and the Morey-Doyle softboard. Doyle was a surfer in love with riding waves, and he got that thrill wherever he could, going back to 1955.

I was skateboarding from 1955 on. We were using metal wheels.

We went on hills that we thought we could make. There was not much turning. The streets were too rough for the metal wheels, so we had to stick to the sidewalk: downhill runs, and the thrill was trying to make the corner without slipping out and having to bail out in the ivy parkway—if you were lucky enough to have ivy.

I always wonder even today how we survived—what if we landed on an upright sprinkler?

My driveway was called "Little Waimea," and to take it on an angle and make a four-inch drop at the bottom and come out on the sidewalk and not the grass was a real challenge.

crates and the T-bars off their scooters, or they nailed those ubiquitous roller skates to a 2x4, and made a machine that would allow them two hands to get their boards to the beach.

From the viewpoint of the twenty-first century looking back on the skateboards of the 1950s, it's amazing anyone survived: metal roller-skate wheels attached to low-tech trucks, nailed or sometimes screwed to thick pieces of wood; no kicktails, no copers, nothing fancy whatsoever. Skateboarding was in its infancy in the 1950s, and the skateboards themselves were infantile.

This is how kids rolled in 1944. Skateboards were just around the corner. *Photo Getty Images. circa 1945*

Pat and Mike O'Neill, circa 1959, skateboarding in front of their dad's surf shop in Santa Cruz. The shop was on the corner of West Cliff Drive and Beach Street. *Courtesy Pat O'Neill*

SIDEWALK SURFING PIONEERS

PETER PARKIN AND CARL KNOX GO SKATEBOARDING, 1947

Peter Parkin and Carl Knox were two La Jolla surfers who first began tinkering with skateboards as a way to get to their surf spot in 1947. Parkin may have been the true instigator of riding two trucks and four wheels attached to a piece of wood down the hills of La Jolla. Knox, now in his seventies, remembered the times.

Peter Parkin was the first one I ever knew to make a skateboard. The only thing that I had ever seen before was a board with a little box on it, with a stick across the top for a handle like a scooter. But the first skateboard I ever saw was made by Peter Parkin.

Peter Parkin lived on Nautilus Street, in La Jolla. We started surfing together when we were around thirteen years old—around 1947, somewhere in that neighborhood—and we used to go to the beach every day. We'd go to Windansea and go surfing. I used to go to his house almost every day.

Anyway, one day I went to his house and he'd made this skateboard. Actually he became very proficient on it—very fast—and it was just a piece of 2x4 about twenty inches long. He'd gone up to the Salvation Army and gotten some older metal roller skates and put them on a sidewalk and pounded them flat with a hammer. Then he put them on a 2x4 and nailed it on there with some eight-penny nails and bent them over. We didn't even use screws.

He made the very first one and he said, "Well, let's go up to the Salvation Army. They get those skates in all the time, and you can make one." He had the perfect place to skate, down Nautilus Street, because it had just a very slight incline toward the beach and he used to skate down there every day.

Anyway, we went to the Salvation Army and we got some more skates, and we used to go up there frequently and get skates. There were some fancy kind of skates that had kind of a round center that were much harder to make the skateboards out of . . . .

We were always looking for the old ones that were flat—with just a little heel cup. We would flatten the heel cups out, and then the ones with the wings on the front, flatten those out, and put them on the 2x4 and pound the nails into them. Actually, considering, they held up pretty well for quite a while.

Carl Knox holding a photo of himself shooting the shorebreak, somewhere in La Jolla, sometime in the 1950s.
Lucia Daniella Griggi

MYTHS, LEGENDS, RUMORS, AND LIES

WHAT WAS THE FIRST COMMERCIALLY PRODUCED SKATEBOARD?

The answer is: We may never know. Many inventors and corporations are quick to stake a claim, but finding that first commercially produced skateboard may be a futile search.

In the first edition of the *Quarterly Skateboarder*, a full-page ad by Skee Skate of California makes a heavy claim: "This is it!!!! The skateboard that started it all."

Others beg to differ. Many historians and collectors believe the eponymous skateboard launched by the Roller Derby Skate Corporation was the first mass-produced skateboard. It well may be, although no one is certain when it was launched.

The Roller Derby was a wooden plank with a rounded tip at one end and modified roller-skate steel wheels attached. It boasted no concave or even kicktail, not to mention grip tape, but it did have a snazzy bright-red paint scheme.

Many believe the Roller Derby made its debut in 1959. But the company itself claims it introduced the board in 1963. David Kennedy, Roller Derby's current vice president and CFO in

Above: An ad for the Skee Skate that boldly appeared in the first issue of the *Quarterly Skateboarder* in 1964. Was this the first commercial skateboard? *Courtesy Surfer Publishing Group*

Left: Top and bottom views of the Humco Surfer, which got all high tech with a spring-loaded suspension. *Humco courtesy G&S*

Red scare! The early skateboard industry apparently saw red as the color of choice for the first skateboards. Red is fast. Red is sexy. Red is good. Red sells. The Skee Skate was one of the earliest mass-produced skateboards. *Courtesy Paul Naude/Billabong*

The Roller Derby, one of the first mass-produced skateboards offered. *Courtesy Paul Naude/ Billabong*

Litchfield, Illinois, responded to this important query by producing a nine-page Roller Derby skateboard promotional brochure—first published in 1964.

Jim Scheller was Roller Derby vice president at the time. He began working for the company in 1957: "I don't recall any skateboards in 1959. I believe that the first skateboard production for Roller Derby was in late 1963 and the beginning of 1964. The idea came from California, where we had a warehouse managed by a guy named Sloniger. We did a little retooling at the plant in Litchfield but not much, and it turned out to be a good business. Very good." While the Roller Derby may not have been the first commercially produced skateboard, it was likely the first *mass*-produced board, as many of them survive today.

Still, other skateboards may have arrived earlier. Historian Iain Borden claims in his *Skateboard, Space and the City: Art and the Body* (2001) that 1956 was the first year: "The first commercial skateboards—like the Humco five-ply deck with 'Sidewalk Swinger' spring-loaded trucks (1956), the Sport Flite, and the Roller Derby (late 1950s to early 1960s)—came with steel wheels around 50mm in diameter and 10mm wide."

In his book *Skateboard Retrospective: A Collector's Guide*, Rhyn Noll points out a two-wheeled contraption from the 1930s owned by Randy Beck from Chatsworth, California. This machine has two wheels attached to a piece of wood, but if we're using the strict definition of four wheels and two trucks, this doesn't quite fit in.

Noll also mentions a Mr. Carl Jensen: "I hear tales of Mr. Carl Jensen in the late fifties, a man who built early skateboards and brought them into my dad's shop, Greg Noll Surfboards. Greg recalls Mr. Jensen as the first to sell skateboards to his Hermosa Beach shop in 1958, and considers him a founder of the commercial skateboard." The book also points to 1958 as the year A. C. Boyden "better known as Humco, patented one of the earliest recognizable skateboards."

Looking through the collections of Todd Huber, Paul Naude, Gordon & Smith, and others, there are numerous odd-looking skateboards—some made of metal, some made of wood—that seem to have come out of the 1950s. There are boards by the Chicago Roller Skate Company, and it would make sense that it would be among the first to manufacture a skateboard, as it was one of the Big Four that controlled roller-skate production in the 1950s.

So which came first? Skee Skate? Roller Derby? Chicago? Humco? Or that Carl Jensen chap? I talked with Greg Noll, who made a good argument that Carl Jensen was the first guy to make a commercial skateboard—and Noll himself may have been there at the start as well.

Now, I don't really care about this all that much and I don't want to go around claiming that I made the first commercial boards, but first of all, in the 1950s we called those boards "bun boards," because when you fell you were always busting your ass.

I opened my first shop on Pacific Coast Highway across from Center Street School in Hermosa Beach. At the time there was this guy Jensen who had five or six guys rolling around on the strand on the north side of the Hermosa Beach pier, riding these boards that had old roller-skate equipment with steel wheels.

Jensen brought them to the shop and said, "This is going to be a good thing." Well, I got so tired of hearing all this BS, but I put a couple in the showcase and they sold. So then I started making some outlines and laminating them and I had a rubber stamp that said "Greg Noll Surfboards," but all the time I was thinking, "These things will never sell."

I sold maybe fifty of the boards over the course of a year, but I didn't really see the potential in it and as usual I was left standing at the train station as the train was pulling away, because then Hobie and Makaha and Gordon & Smith came along and of course they sold millions of the things—everyone's making a bunch of dough.

I don't have one of those original Greg Noll stamped skateboards and I wish I did. But just this year Element came out with a special edition of those bun boards, and they look pretty much the same as what we were making back there in the late 1950s, early 1960s.

So am I the first guy to make a commercial skateboard? I don't give a damn. All I know is, a lot of guys got rich from something I didn't think was going anywhere.

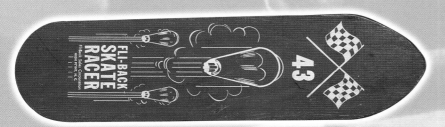

The Fli-Back Sales Corporation of High Point, North Carolina, jumped into the skateboard market with a Skate Racer branded with one of the most famous two-digit numbers in the history of NASCAR–the 43 mark that identified Richard Petty. *Board courtesy Paul Naude/Billabong*

Shark surfboard, made by Nash. *Courtesy the Boardroom*

LIFE

The craze and
the menace of

SKATEBOARDS

San Diego's Pat McGee,
national girls' champion,
does a handstand on wheels

MAY 14 · 1965 · 35¢

Skateboarding goes nationwide: Patti McGee rides
the cover of *Life* magazine on May 14, 1965.

was made like a surfboard, with hard resin and a core. I've never seen such a beautiful skateboard in my life.

Tony Alva and Jay Adams rode on Makaha in the 1970s before Dog Town, and in-between sometimes. And also Bruce Logan and his brothers before Logan Earth Ski. My dad discovered Bruce Logan.

Author: Then everyone jumped ship from the Makaha team to Hobie at some point in the 1960s. That seems kind of disloyal.

CS: Well they paid better.

Author: Is that it?

CS: Yeah. My dad was a lifeguard; they had Conrad Hilton's money.

Author: No hard feelings with Hobie?

CS: Hobie said that Larry Stevenson was the first person he saw put out a modern-day skateboard. There is no question that Larry was the first guy to really embrace skateboarding and bring kids, get them on the team. He had the first contests.

Author: Was that first at Pier Avenue?

CS: It's a debate whether it was in Hermosa at Pier or right here down at Bay Street in Santa Monica. I think there were a couple of them, and they get confused. I think there were a couple of them that same year, 1963.

Author: How did Larry market Makaha originally?

CS: *Surf Guide* was how he marketed Makaha, period.

Author: Anywhere else?

CS: Joe Hammond was one of dad's friends who was a sporting goods rep. Joe went to all the sporting goods shows around the country. And he went to the National Sporting Goods Association [NSGA] show in Chicago in 1963 and came back with a thousand-board order. He goes "Larry, you know you've got the next Hula Hoop? You need to start making these things right now, you've got orders." And that's when everything really took off . . .

I mean there were only two people really making good skateboards. It was Makaha at first, then Hobie. My dad got the jump on everybody and was able to really make a killing at the NSGA show. Of course next year everyone else was there with their own versions of skateboards too. People now don't realize how big skateboarding really was in the 1960s. It was an explosion from 1963 to 1965.

Author: Did you guys make your own trucks or wheels?

CS: He had to get all of his stuff from Chicago Roller Skates in the early days, or else he couldn't have the apparatus, trucks, wheels, and bearings. He actually drove there to Chicago to get the stuff and bring it back. But then he started making his own wheels and all of his own stuff here in Santa Monica.

Author: Did he make his own trucks?

CS: Stamped metal trucks, with a baseplate and a hangar that housed the axle. So he didn't really have to buy trucks, he was being held hostage by the roller-skate companies. Then in the early 1970s he went to China and started getting all kinds of skateboard trucks made. He was one of the first guys to go over to Taipei and Taiwan and get boards. He had some of the coolest boards. You know, I remember sitting in a hotel room with him over there, designing skateboards when I was like nine years old. The Chinese now have their own skateboard companies. But really the first person to import skateboards from China was Larry Stevenson. It's not something we're totally proud of, because some of the boards weren't that great. But we are proud of the fact that the sales that he attained really helped him move him along in his life.

A Makaha ad introducing the idea of sidewalk surfing, from the March 1964 issue of *Surf Guide*. *Courtesy Larry Stevenson*

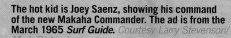

The hot kid is Joey Saenz, showing his command of the new Makaha Commander. The ad is from the March 1965 *Surf Guide*. *Courtesy Larry Stevenson/ Mark Richards*

Mike Hynson does his famous surfing soul arch aboard a Makaha skateboard for this November 1963 ad.

LARRY GORDON AND THE ORIGIN OF THE FIBREFLEX

FIBREFLEX
SKATEBOARD
by
GORDON SMITH

Larry Gordon with a left handful of original 1950s art, and a 1960s improvement in his right hand.
Lucia Daniella Griggi

Larry Gordon is the G in Gordon & Smith, also known as G&S. Gordon is one of the pillars of the surf industrial complex. He branched off into skateboarding in the 1960s and became a pillar of that as well. G&S introduced the FibreFlex board, which became one of the most popular skateboards out of the 1960s into the 1970s.

In 1964, Gordon applied surfboard technology to skateboards. He took a fiberglass-reinforced epoxy called Bo-Tuff and blended it with a maple wood core to make the first laminated deck. Bo-Tuff was truly tough stuff, used to make archery bows that set new records for shooting arrows over a mile. The deck was also arched, which added to its springiness. G&S named its deck the FibreFlex for its responsive ride.

G&S is one of the longest-running companies in surfing and skateboarding—and they are still going strong. In October 2009, the company celebrated its fiftieth anniversary. Among the skateboard set, Mike Hynson, Skip Frye, Henry Hester, Stacy Peralta, and Doug Saladino were there to thank Larry Gordon.

Author: During the 1960s, it seemed like most skateboards were made of wood, but Gordon & Smith was one of the first to get into plastics.

Larry Gordon [LS]: We were experimenting with a fiberglass and epoxy resin that had been used to make a bow that could shoot an arrow for a mile. Seemed like a good material.

My dad worked as a chemist during the war. They had a chemist and a physicist in the R&D department who developed new kinds of fiberglass and different uses for fiberglass. When the war was over, they started a company that made the first fishing poles.

They saturated the fiberglass with the epoxy resin, and it was mostly a longitudinal type weave, so most of the strength was the one way, not much the other way . . . I just kind of intuitively had a feeling they'd make a nice board, for slalom especially.

Author: Where were you getting the raw material? Were you producing the fiberglass, or the sheets?

LS: We bought the sheets from my dad. We could do any width up to a foot wide. So most of them at that time, the first boards we made in 1964 were probably about 6 to 7 inches wide.

Author: Were you skateboarding in the 1950s on crummy pieces of wood?

LS: Yeah. That was kind of the thing that went around the neighborhood. Every few years we'd get a 2x4, get an adjustable skate, and we'd take the two parts and nail it on, and we had a skateboard.

The 1963 to 1964 period is when skateboarding had the potential to be a sport. All the top surfers would meet and do slalom races up in Laguna Beach and here in La Costa.

So in 1964 we decided we had a better idea for the skateboard and we called it the FibreFlex. We started making them, and we made about a thousand of them, and then everything stopped. They had the first Anaheim U.S. contest, and Gordon & Smith had a team in that, and we did really good and we thought we were on the way.

Author: G&S team members Willie Nelson and Skip Frye finished first and second in Downhill Slalom. The G&S team finished second to Hobie Super Surfer Southern California.

LS: But then the publicity was pretty bad. Every little thing that happened, it seemed like it was blown out of proportion.

Author: So you came in kind of late in 1964 in the middle of the boom. You say you only made 1,000 boards?

LS: Yeah. We called them a Surf-Skate. They didn't have the urethane wheels; they were clay.

Author: Did you lose money when skateboarding bombed in 1965?

LS: Oh, I'm sure we lost a little bit, yeah. We bought equipment and we were kind of geared up to. . . we had all our presses. We didn't lose that much.

Author: Did you just completely stop making them after 1965?

LS: Yeah, until about 1975. And then those years 1976, 1977, 1978, they were incredible. In fact, I think one of those years when the skateboard thing peaked, that was our best year ever.

Author: How did that come about?

LS: Well we had a couple boards from the 1960s laying around in the office, you know how that is. You have your junky corner, and it sits there, and it sits there, and we moved. And my office still had a bunch of junk in it. And then about 1975 my cousin said, "Let's make those FibreFlex skateboards again, things are heating up!" And I go, "Nah we couldn't sell all the ones that we made. . ." He said, "Let me. Let me try to make 'em in my garage, and if we sell 'em we'll go into that business."

I go, "Well that sounds reasonable." So we started making skateboards in his garage and he never did get caught up with the orders. We were buried.

Author: Basically the same board from 1964 to 1975? Same material?

LS: Yeah, same material. Our best year was about 1977 or 1978—we did six million dollars in skateboards alone.

Author: You made more money from skateboards than surfboards?

LS: Yeah, oh yeah.

A FibreFlex ad featuring Mike Hynson, from the Magazine Formerly Known as the *Quarterly Skateboarder*, which became *SkateBoarder* magazine for the third issue.
Courtesy Surfer Publishing Group

A collection of G&S Fibreflexes from the 1960s and 1970s from the Gordon and Smith Collection.

THE ENDLESS CONCRETE

HOBIE SKATEBOARDS AND BRUCE BROWN'S *ENDLESS SUMMER* TOUR

In 1964, California surf-movie maker Bruce Brown was appalled by how his beloved sport was being depicted in the mainstream. *Gidget*, Frankie and Annette, the Beach Boys—most of the words and images were phony, and the square world was cashing in on what had been a secret thrill.

Bruce Brown had been a serious moviemaker before surfing became popular, and in 1964 he set out on an around-the-world trip with two well-groomed, well-dressed, respectable young surfers to make a documentary that detailed the realities of the surfing lifestyle to the squares: "Real surfers don't break into song in front of their girlfriends!"

Bruce Brown's *Endless Summer* was a smash hit, the most successful documentary produced up to 1964. There wasn't really any skateboarding in *Endless Summer*, but by the time the movie came out, the skateboard sensation was sweeping the nation.

In 1964, Hobie teamed up with Bruce Brown's *Endless Summer* tour. In this story, excerpted from the *Surfer's Journal* by kind permission of Steve Pezman, Hobie Alter remembered the tour.

That's where the Endless Summer *tour came in, in 1964. I'd seen Bruce's movie and it was* really *good, so I asked him if I could put together a run down the East Coast, giving surfing demonstrations and doing eight showings. I'd cover all the costs. We'd split the take with the local shops that put on the showings. Bruce had his premiere showing in a theater on Hollywood Blvd. and then he got on a plane to Oklahoma City to catch up with us. We were driving non-stop. In three days we were in New York. We had a big Ford Condor bus with Bruce and Pat [Brown], Phil and Heidi [Edwards], Corky [Carroll], Mike Hynson, Joey Cabell, Sharon [Hobie's first wife], and me. We packed*

20,000 people at Gilgo Beach. We'd sent R. Paul Allen ahead to set up and get the PR going, and then we'd pull in with the bus. It was fun. Joey bailed out in New Jersey and then Bruce flew home after the last show in Miami. Phil and I did most of the driving. Corky wasn't old enough, but I think I let him drive some open road. In New York, Paul had arranged to get us on The Tonight Show *starring Johnny Carson. We had the first skateboards with us in 1964. Corky rode one on TV!*

Now backing up just a little bit. Larry Stevenson started Makaha Skateboards, and he is the one that kicked off the big skateboarding fad. He had the team riders and the clay wheels—real skateboards. All of us had skated on 2x4s with roller skate wheels and the box nailed on the front, but the first real skateboard was from Larry. I get credit for stealing his team. Originally I was going to make them and then Barron Hilton called me. His kids, Davey, Stevie, and Barron were skateboarding Santa Monica with George Trafton and Torger Johnson—all those hot surfer guys—and Barron owned Vita-Pakt, an orange juice company in Covina, along with a few hotels. They made the Super Skater, a roller skate that broke apart and clamped back together to make a skateboard. It was a hot little item with kids but they wanted to make real skateboards, using my name, and I said fine. I was just getting ready to do it myself but it was a blessing that I didn't, and so I got a royalty from that. The first skateboards arrived the day before we left on the bus trip. None of us were familiar with skateboards, so we became acquainted with them on the trip. Every gas station we stopped at we checked for the quality of the asphalt. Nobody had seen it. One place in South Carolina (it was during the time of the Civil Rights movement down there) people wondered if we're part of it: "No, we're surfers."

THE LINDA BENSON SIGNATURE MODEL SKATEBOARD

From left: L.J. Richards, Linda Benson, and Don Hansen in January 2010. *Lucia Daniella Griggi*

Linda Benson was one of the first female surf stars. She was a flashy, goofy-foot surfer, and the fifteen-year-old winner of the 1959 Makaha International—a true hot-dogger.

In 1961–1966, Benson surfed for surfboard shaper Don Hansen. Hansen later created a skateboard to Benson's specs, christened the Linda Benson Signature Model skateboard.

Author: Was the Linda Benson skateboard the first signature model?
Linda Benson [LB]: I think it was the first women's signature model.
Author: When did you start skateboarding?
LB: It must have been 1964.
Author: You were never on metal wheels and things like that?
LB: Yes, we made skateboards with the metal wheels you pulled apart, then nailed them on 2x4s. We could adjust the play so they would turn better.

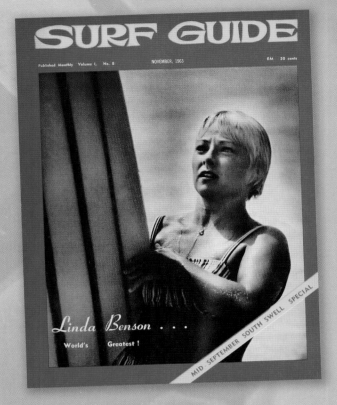

SURF GUIDE

Published Monthly Volume I, No. 8   NOVEMBER, 1963   RM 50 cents

Linda Benson . . .

World's   Greatest !

MID SEPTEMBER SOUTH SWELL SPECIAL

Linda Benson on the cover of *Surf Guide.*
Courtesy Val Surf/Larry Stevenson

Linda Benson with one of her Hansen model skateboards. Lucia Daniella Griggi

Author: Did you really skateboard a lot?

LB: We did it because we were surfers, and we did it when there was no surf.

Author: When did the signature models come out?

LB: It was all before 1964.

Author: Did you actually assemble the boards?

LB: Yes I did. I screwed those wheels on the back rim. By hand. No drill.

Author: How many would you do?

LB: I would put together maybe a hundred, and then load 'em in my little red '57 Triumph and drive up to Los Angeles—Santa Monica. That was a big trip back then.

And so I went up to Santa Monica, but there were no sporting goods at the time. It was either Pep Boys or hardware stores, because they carried balls and bats and sporting goods. I went around to these stores and I'd go in and say "Hey I have a new product. But I have to show you how it works." So we'd go outside to the sidewalk and I'd demonstrate it and they'd take a few.

Don paid for a hotel room so I wouldn't have to come back. I must have been nineteen, but I would get so tired. Not from skateboarding; I think it was from driving around in the big city trying to find these stores and parking spaces.

Author: How fast would those boards sell?

LB: Well, people were intrigued. But I think they were probably a little bit leery to put them in the store, because there they are, a little surfboard with wheels on it. And what do you really do with it? So probably they didn't fly off the shelves immediately.

Author: But this was when skateboarding was booming, it was popular, people knew about it. It was in *Life* magazine.

LB: This was before the boom. People that didn't surf didn't know anything about this.

Author: Not the nation.

LB: No, uh-uh.

Author: Did you do demonstrations?

LB: The Art Linkletter Show. We went out to NBC, ABC, whatever it was. We were out in the parking lot and that's where we demonstrated the skateboards.

Author: Did you make any money? Do you remember?

LB: Oh you made money. . . couple hundred dollars.

COVER GIRL

PATTI MCGEE, SKATEBOARDING'S FIRST IT GIRL

Patti McGee graces the cover of the *Skaterboarder Magazine*.

In 1965, Patti McGee was skateboarding's reigning queen. She appeared on the cover of *Life* magazine's May 14, 1965, issue, which was as big as national media exposure got back then. Patti also appeared on the final cover of *Quarterly Skateboarder*, an equally big deal in the world of skateboarding.

Author: You won the First Annual National Skateboard Championships on January 3, 1965, in Santa Monica?

Patti McGee [PM]: Yes. It was conducted at the Santa Monica Civic Auditorium by the recreation and parks department. There were eighty-four kids that competed. I was the Women's National Champion. Danny Bearer was the Men's National Champion, and Michael Mel won the Boy's division. I rode for the Bun Buster team then, and had done a few demos with my brother, Jack McGee, plus a big one in Denver for Walt Disney.

Author: What divisions were there?

PM: They had the girls and boys in separate divisions. Although I tied with Danny Bearer with my points, I never got to share the trophy with Makaha. I would love to have my picture taken with it after all these years.

Author: Do you remember what the events were?

PM: There were three: slalom, jump, and freestyle . . . I don't recall doing the over the bar jump, but it was one of our best tricks we did on tour. I was really good at it!

Slalom was a time trial with cones—that was fun.

There was the figure eight, and that knocked a lot of people out because they did a pattern like the infinity sign, and that's not a figure eight.

Author: Did they have that traced out on the pavement?

PM: ; No, I just knew it. I roller figure skated when I was younger, rink-style, with jumps and spins and figure eights: a figure eight is two complete circles, back to center.

Author: How many times could you push for speed?

PM: One time in the center to start as you went out and around to make the first circle, and then again as you came back through the center to complete the second circle.

Freestyle let everybody shine. I'm only guessing, but I think we had two to three minutes to impress the judges. The tricks then were no big deal compared to today's standards. We did a series of 180s, like walking the deck on its wheels into a smooth series of 360s. We did wheelies and nose wheelies. Walking up, foot over foot, and hanging five or ten. That's when I turned loose my handstand, which became my signature trick. If I knew then what I know now! I would have blown them all away, huh? We all would have.

Author: How did they judge that?

PM: The whole event was judged by the flip of the cards, like swimming or ice-skating: tossing the high and low and averaging out the three remaining scores. They all added together for your grand total.

Author: So tell me about these skateboards and trophies you so kindly brought.

PM: This is the trophy from the 1965 National in Santa Monica. This is the Vita-Pakt trophy that I took to all the appearances. I did a lot of events. I traveled all over the United States doing events for Hobie Skateboards as their sales rep. Whenever I could I would have a little event, and this would be the trophy that I would give out.

Author: Introduce your quiver of skateboards.

PM: This is the Hobie laminated—my original board. Then the Challenger, by Bun Buster. My G&S. The Hobie Super Surfer. A Hobie fiberglass and a Bun Buster by Cooley. These are all my original boards from forty-six years ago. Bun Buster was my first

team, and that was the board that I rode into the 1965 Nationals. The Challenger was also a Bun Buster product. It was just a longer version—more of a cruising model and great for the over the bar jump.

Author: Tell me about riding for Bun Buster and George Cooley.

PM: George Cooley was from Manhattan Beach, and he had his warehouse there when they got their first order for some drugstore. They actually got the order before they had the boards, and had to scramble. Good thing Geo had a connection with the Chicago wheel guy.

We had cool team jackets—I still have mine!—and a few boards each. Our biggest booth was at the 1964 Dick Clark's World Teen Fair at the Orange County fairgrounds over Easter vacation. We would skate all over our large area and talk to folks and show off the boards. Somebody got the harebrained idea to get a water-ski rope outta the back of my VW bus and get us towed out in the parking lot. I've got to say it wasn't one of the brightest things I dreamed up, since I rode barefoot and safety gear was still in the box.

Author: And what about the Hobies you rode?

PM: The Hobie board was their classic laminate. They came out with the Super Surfer in late 1963, early 1964, and it was more of their Montgomery Ward production board. And then we've got the fiberglass model—sweet. They came out with it in 1965. Everything

A Cooley ad from *Quarterly Skateboarder* issue two.
Courtesy Val Surf/Surfer Publishing Group

Skateboarding as participation toy: an ad from the third issue of *SkateBoarder* magazine.
Courtesy Surfer Publishing Group

Patti McGee in Malibu, showing off trophies, boards, jackets, and other memorabilia from her years as skateboarding's it girl in the mid-1960s. *Ben Marcus*

GRAND OPENING LABOR DAY WEEKEND
FRIDAY, SEPT. 3 thru MONDAY, SEPT. 6, 9 A.M. till 12 P.M.

SURF CITY
"WORLD'S FIRST" CHAMPIONSHIP SKATEBOARD COURSE
5140 E. SPEEDWAY

SEE Marshal KGUN Shoot the CURL FRI. NIGHT — Friday SEE PAT McGEE — SEE Dr. Scar & Mr. Buttercrunch Saturday and Sunday

FREE PRIZES SKATEBOARDS & BULLFIGHT TICKETS

Bring Your Own Skateboard If it Has Composition Wheels or We Will Rent You One.

Safety Helmets Provided FREE For Every Skateboarder

PAT McGEE Life Cover Girl & Champion Skateboarder

Rubber Sole Shoes Only If You Don't Have Them, We'll Rent Them Too!

ADMISSION SKATE AS LONG AS YOU LIKE $1
SPECTATORS . . . only 25¢

No year on this poster for the Surf City skateboard park in Tucson, Arizona, but if it's 1965, then it's before Surfer's World in Anaheim. *Visual courtesy Patti McGee/Scott Starr*

happened really fast. It happened within a year and a half, and then it just kinda went by the wayside for a while. Mostly due to the insurance factors and bad press.

Author: Were you surfing before you were skateboarding?

PM: Yes, I started surfing in 1958 in Ocean Beach, San Diego, on an old balsa Burlan. But I also sailed and swam for the San Diego Yacht Club.

Author: How were you exposed to skateboarding?

PM: My little brother swiped the clay wheels off my rink skates and bolted them down on a plank he made in woodshop. I started skateboarding right at the end of high school, in 1963. I tried that board my brother Jack put together out in our driveway, but my first real board was a Bun Buster.

Author: Were there other girls skateboarding?

PM: Nope! Well, perhaps casually, but I was the devoted daredevil in San Diego—my skateboard traveled with me wherever I went. I was pretty much a free spirit and did what was the most radical thing to do at the time.

Author: What was your skateboarding experience before you became a competitor and professional?

PM: We just went wild, you might say. Anything to get to the thrill of it all. Always looking for a steep hill, of course, and they had just started building the notorious parking lot buildings. Yipppeeeee!

Author: I think I saw that building in *Quarterly Skateboarder*. That was the circular building with twelve levels, that Mike Hynson and them were skateboarding?

PM: More than likely. We rode it in different stages as it got built and were always getting chased. The whole purpose every day was to blast on through somewhere and not get caught.

Author: Were you in other contests before the Santa Monica Nationals?

PM: No, that was my first and only. Once I was on the payroll at Vita-Pakt I lost my amateur standing and wasn't allowed to compete. Besides, I was on tour on the East Coast at the time. Better to get paid at the time, cause now I was almost twenty.

Author: Did Hobie steal you away from Bun Buster?

PM: No, I showed up at Hobie's surf shop in Dana Point in my old 1956 VW bus with my trophy and a fistful of glossy 8x10s—the afternoon he was headed to New York to line up a California promotion with Macy's Department Store and the Montgomery Ward Stores. I have always felt that five more minutes and I would have missed him, and everything would have been different. Poooof!

Author: Where did you go on these tours, and what did you do?

PM: The first place they sent me was east to New York. I went as an executive. I had to wear a gray pleated skirt and a blue blazer and heels—ouch! If you look at the *Life* magazine and look really close at the heels of my feet, you'll see the Band-Aids from my fancy shoes. I skated barefoot, so shoes killed my feet.

So then, I got into New York. What a trip that was for a barefoot California surfer girl. The first day I actually started out with our rep, who was the big toy rep for Tonka at the Fifth Avenue Toy Building. The taxicabs wouldn't pick me up because I was wearing shorts and a Vita-Pakt orange velour V-neck, carrying a board with wheels on it, and barefooted. I'm serious.

Guess it was the next day after that I got the call from the Macy's Department event lady and she said that *Life* magazine was a go. They sent me a limo, because now they knew I was going to be *on the cover of* Life!

They also had lined up *What's My Line?*, because I had to be on Sunday before the magazine broke and hit the stands on Monday. I could hardly contain myself, because Johnny Carson was the following night. My head was in a spin. It was all happening so fast.

Then I would fly to Tucson and make a personal appearance for the opening of the skatepark in 1965. That summer I did the whole Montgomery Ward tour through Oregon and Washington.

I chaperoned the whole Hobie Team for a national television personal appearance at the San Diego Chargers halftime on Thanksgiving 1965.

Author: Were they paying you well?

PM: Compared to what? I was on salary with Vita-Pakt. I got paid about three hundred dollars a month, plus all expenses. I had to make a living too, because I had Volkswagen bus car payments, [and] I needed a new surfboard.

Things kept rolling until spring 1966. I shipped out for another Dick Clark World Teen Fair, this time in Chicago at the Stockyard Inn and Convention Centers. My booth at this event was enormous, and I had fifty skateboards hanging up and all the trophies on display.

I did a contest twice a day for the whole spring break, then a final contest at the end. Every rock 'n' roll group you can think of at that time was there, except the Beatles and the Stones: we had Frankie Valli, and the Young Rascals, and Sonny and Cher. We all stayed on the same floor of the Inn. Talk about party all night! The music never stopped: upstairs, downstairs, on the stairs, and in the halls. The main stage played to forty-five thousand kids.

But that was the end of the touring—summer 1966. There were still some appearances and interviews, but for the most part my job was done with Vita-Pakt.

Making the covers of *Life* and *Skateboarder* didn't have much impact on my life for many years—until my daughter asked if she could interview me for her college communications class. That spurred a screen-printing endeavor and a website, www.FirstBetty. com, and a clothing line with some of my old photos for the graphics.

I was contacted one afternoon in 2002-ish by two of skateboarding's bad boys: Dave Hackett and Steve Olson. That call changed my life too: Dave and I made a trade, a Deathbox deck for my autographed zine covers.

So I started skating again at fifty-four years old.

With clay wheels came the search for the perfect riding surface. In the 1960s, a crew of skaters found their skateboard paradise at a newly opened parking garage overlooking San Diego Harbor. This is from the second issue of the *Quarterly Skateboarder*.
Courtesy Surfer Publishing Group

THE DEVIL'S TOY

CANADIAN KIDS GET WILD IN THE STREET

In 1966, perhaps inspired by the award-winning *Skaterdater*, the National Film Board of Canada and director Claude Jutra teamed up to make their own short skateboarding documentary.

The Devil's Toy sounds pretty stern, but in fact the movie is a tongue-in-cheek indictment not of skateboarding, but of cops and cities demonizing skateboarding and passing laws to make skateboarding illegal.

The National Film Board of Canada described *The Devil's Toy* in their website: "It was frowned upon by the constabulary and disapproving adults, but the skateboard gave the youngsters who mastered its technique a thrilling sensation of speed unexcelled by any other pavement sport. Filmed in 1966 on Montreal streets before the elongated roller skate was banned, this film captures the exuberance of boys and girls having the time of their lives in free-wheeling downhill locomotion."

The storyline is simpler than *Skaterdater*. Ominous music, the subtitle "this film is dedicated to all victims of intolerance," and a stern-voiced narrator begins the movie with tones of gloom and doom: "These are the remains of what was once a beautiful city.

But the mind of man is as rich in evil as it is in good. And the same inventiveness which blessed us with insulin, electricity, the arts, and engineering miracles of all sorts, has also cursed us with the sword, the gun, the bomb, and . . ."

A skateboard shaped with a dangerously pointy nose rolls into view, with a skull-and-crossbones graphic that predates Powell-Peralta by about fifteen years. Innocent families and baby ducks are shown enjoying a fine fall day in a Montreal park, while the narrator continues: "For it was like a plague which spread from city to city, an epidemic from which no one was secure. A dread disease, which needed only pavement to multiply and proliferate."

To the screaming wails of the undead, a group of skater kids are shown getting wild in the streets of Montreal, doing the tricks the surfers do, getting rousted by the cops, and then getting their boards back when they agree to skate only on the wooden floor of an unfrozen ice rink.

The Devil's Toy didn't get nominated for awards at Cannes, but in 1968 it did win a Gold Plaque in the category of Films for Youth 14 and 15 Years Old at the International Festival of Films for Children and Young Adults in Tehran, Iran. It also won a Special Mention in the Short Films category at the Festival of Canadian Films—Montreal International Film Festival in 1967.

Continued from page 95

to worry about then keeping their ball bearings from falling out. Now they had the "Big Decision" to make about whether to join up and fight an unpopular war, accept the draft, leave the country, possibly for good.

That said, it's not fair to characterize 1965–1970 entirely as the Dark Ages. Kids were still skateboarding, and a lot of the men and women who would go on to pioneer the skateboard industry of later decades took their first rides on a skateboard during this era.

Vans opened their shoe factory in Anaheim in 1966, the same year that the city's public skatepark, Surfer's World, opened. But perhaps the most important innovation of the time came in 1969, when Larry Stevenson of Makaha Skateboards put a bend in the end of a skateboard and invented the kicktail. The kicktail made skateboards easier to maneuver and, most importantly, easier to stop. Improvements in skateboard trucks and other components laid down a foundation for the revolution that was just around the corner: plastics.

Continued on page 103

Despite the best efforts of pop crooner Tom Jones, skateboarding didn't catch on in the late 1960s. *Michael Ochs Archive/Getty Images*

HOBIE 1966

CRIS DAWSON ILLUMINATES THE DARK AGES

Now a graphic designer, Cris Dawson was a player in the 1960s and 1970s, during the transition from clay wheels to urethane. *Lucia Daniella Griggi*

Cris Dawson skated for the Hobie Super Surfer skateboard team in the late 1960s. He remembers the so-called Dark Ages as not being so dark.

Cris Dawson [CD]: During the 1960s, I was doing like thirty 360s on one of those older, clay-wheeled boards.

Author: Thirty?

CD: Yeah. Headstands, handstands. All the other things that everybody was doing at that time. We were doing headstands, handstands, and something called the Dewey Walk, which is a super-speed walk [that] nobody knows about.

Author: It was a big deal to get on the Hobie team.

CD: It was a huge deal to be on the Hobie team.

Author: So they did a whole new team? All these guys were gone?

CD: Whole new team.

Author: So what did it take to get on the team?

CD: There was a contest that was at Pacific Palisades High School, and there were three guys: myself, Tommy Waller, and Ray Flores, and we were from the Mar Vista area. We heard about the contest and we went up to the contest, and we took first, second, and third and the

promotion guy was there and he said, "I've got my team!"

Author: You three.

CD: Yeah and then there were three women: Wendy Bearer, Colleen Boyd, and Susie Rowland. We were doing exhibitions every weekend all around Southern California. We had the Hobie Gold thing, is what it was all about. They went around to all the different cities and put on competitions. We were the judges.

Author: So skateboarding kept going.

CD: Skateboarding kept going.

Author: It wasn't really the Dark Ages.

CD: No, it wasn't. As far as the manufacturers go, they thought it was the Dark Ages, because after 1966 everything just sort of . . . shut down. The smaller little skate shops and . . . guys still built boards, but it wasn't on any type of a national basis.

Author: And Hobie was still going, though? They were still selling boards?

CD: Yeah I think so. They didn't have the large production, but they were still making boards.

Author: How long were you on the team?

CD: We were basically on the team for about one year.

Author: Did they come up with a new team every year or did they . . .

CD: After that I don't think they came up with another team.

Author: And then it died. It really did just die.

CD: It really did die, yeah.

Author: So you are from Mar Vista. When did you start skateboarding?

CD: Oh I started skateboarding probably . . . in 1958?

Author: Metal wheels?

CD: Metal wheels, a 2x4 with nailed-on wheels.

Author: How did you ride those boards? They were terrible!

CD: We went straight, most of the time. The most important thing that we did back then was to see how our agility was on riding on the curb. So we got the grass and this little curb that was about that wide. And we'd see how far we could go down.

Author: Was clay as big a leap from metal as urethane was to clay?

CD: I think it was . . . the clay wheels were part of roller skating at that time, but not so much for the younger guys who were at home who just had the strap-on skates. They took the strap-on skates and then they put them on the 2x4s with an orange crate on it. The

orange crate did fall off, and then we rode without the orange crate. It was just much better.

Author: So after you were off the Hobie team, did you stop skateboarding?

CD: Yeah then I went to college. I went to the Chouinard Art Institute and then I went to Cal Arts. I still skateboarded . . . but nothing really amazing. And then in 1975 I got a knock on my door, you know, and someone said, "Skateboarding's back!" So that's when I joined the Zephyr team.

Author: A knock from who?

CD: Tommy Waller.

Author: Tommy Waller knocked on the door. . .

CD: And said, "Skateboarding's back!" I went to a competition in Huntington Beach and they wouldn't let me be a part of the competition because I hadn't registered the day before. So I got to do an exhibition.

Author: Freestyle?

CD: Freestyle, yeah.

Author: How many 360s could you do then?

CD: I could probably do fifteen or twenty.

Hobie Super Surfer Model 1468.
Courtesy Cris Dawson

RUBBER SOLE

VANS EMERGES IN ANAHEIM

Vans was not the first company to make skateboard shoes, but Vans rose from perhaps the first company to do it.

Paul van Doren was an employee of the Randolph Rubber Company (also known as Randy's) in Boston for twenty years, eventually working his way up to executive vice president. In 1964, van Doren loaded up his family and went west to grow with the country—and Randy's. With his brother Jim and friend Gordon Lee, he got the west coast arm of Randy's running profitably. But then van Doren made a risky but fateful decision: to go into the shoe business on his own.

Van Doren wanted his shoe company to have a twist: he wanted to manufacture shoes *and* retail them, because for many years he'd seen companies sell shoes wholesale to retailers for pennies, which retailers would then sell for dollars.

Working again with Jim (who was an engineer), Lee, and Serge D'Ella (who had experience in the shoe business), it took van Doren a year to set up his Anaheim factory. The grand opening was pushed forward a couple of months, and then in March 1966, Vans opened for business at 704 East Broadway in Anaheim. Sixteen customers came in that day, and their shoes were ready the next day.

The van Dorens began making deck shoes, which they sold at swap meets and in their own stores. Vans' shoes were different because they used pure crepe rubber to make soles twice as thick as other shoes on the market. When the soles began to crack, they devised a pattern of nine lines over diamonds on the sole of the shoe, which made them even more bulletproof.

The first Vans sold for $4.99 for mens' shoes and $2.29 for womens'. Customers would order the shoes in the morning and they would be ready by afternoon, although custom orders took longer. Within a year and half, Vans had opened fifty stores, and their success was, in part, because skateboarders discovered that these customizable shoes with the thick rubber soles could handle the rigors of skateboarding: bending, flexing, dragging your toe while doing kickturns.

It wasn't until 1975 that Vans began making shoes specifically for skateboarders—but all of those chances taken in 1966 lit the fuse of something that would blow up into a billion-dollar industry by the turn of the century.

THE OFFICIAL SNEAKER OF THE NATIONAL SKATEBOARD CHAMPIONSHIPS INC.

NSC

FOR SIDEWALK SURFING . . .

Randy "720" SKATEBOARDER Sneaker

WITH TUFF TOE 'N HEEL MADE WITH RANDYPRENE® FOR BUILT IN TUFFNESS

Today's increased performance on Skateboards makes "TUFFER" demands on sneakers than ever before. That's why we're making our outsole "TUFFER" with the all new Randy compound . . . . "RANDYPRENE®, designed with the new Tuff Toe 'N Heel guaranteed to withstand the TUFF treatment given by the Skateboarder. Made by Randy's skilled shoe-makers, with army duck uppers, arch cushioned insole, and steel shank for extra foot comfort. For men, boys and youths in white, navy and loden green.

*TUFF TOE 'N HEEL . . . . A Randy exclusive . . . made with RANDYPRENE® . . . . a combination of Shell Isoprene, the rubber with the built in TUFFNESS, a special compound . . . and Randy knowhow.

Write in for name of nearest dealer . . . Dealer inquiries invited.

QUALITY BY Randy

From coast to coast...

RANDOLPH MFG. CO., INC. • 32 South Main St. • Randolph. Mass.
RANDOLPH RUBBER CO. • 10631 Stanford St. • Garden Grove, Calif.

SKATEBOARDER magazine   3

From the Hobie team in 1966 to Dogtown 1975, Ray Flores is a skateboarder who made the jump from the clay wheels of the 1960s to the plastics revolution of the 1970s.
Lucia Daniella Griggi

Continued from page 99

Craig Stecyk III was surfing and skateboarding in 1968, and he remembers that rumors of the death of skateboarding were highly exaggerated. He believes skateboarding just went underground. "I recall pods of people skateboarding," he says "I remember attending raiding parties forming up at the beach and deploying en masse to go skate at a Beverly Hills parking garage, Revere or something equivalent. The Sorrento–State Beach contingent would have a core makeup of Beaver Smith; Dave, Steve, and Barry Hilton; Danny Bearer; J. Riddle; Torger; plus whoever else happened to be around. The Ocean Park contingent had people in it like Victor Torres, Vincent McGarey, Mike Mishich, Skip Engblom, Wayne Inouye, Michel Junod, Jeff Ho, etcetera."

Perhaps the best thing to come out of this time period was *Skaterdater*, a sixteen-minute movie that used kids skateboarding around the hills of Southern California to tell a coming of age story. *Skaterdater* won two awards at the Cannes Film Festival and was nominated for an Academy Award.

Skaterdater went far beyond anyone's expectations, and if you watch the movie with some knowledge of skateboard history, you'll see that its themes predicted all that was to come in skateboarding: courage, leadership, girls, challenge to leadership, losing innocence, growing up.

So, the mid- to late 1960s wasn't entirely dead for skateboarding In fact, in this relatively quiet period, skateboarding organized itself for a second burst that was just around the corner. And the clue to that can be seen in another movie that came out in 1967 and what was coming can be summed up in one word: "Plastics."

THE KICKTAIL

THE STEVENSONS DETAIL THE GREATEST INNOVATION OF THE DARK AGES

Larry Stevenson, the founder of Makaha Skateboards, survived the Dark Ages by inventing the light at the end of the tunnel. His *Surf Guide* magazine closed shop with the March 1965 issue. Afterward, Larry took some time off to sail around the world. When he returned, a new idea was brimming.

Curt Stevenson [CS]: My father moved to Playa Del Rey, and that's when he started making kicktails. I was about four or five years old when he made a wood mold and he cut it like this, with a bandsaw. And then he separated the halves and drilled giant holes all the way around it to where he could bolt it down, make a clamp. And then he started putting laminates of wood one on one, painting glue on each laminate 'til it was about that thick. And when it was all said and done he came out with a kicktail.

He feels that his invention of the kicktail and the double kicktail helped make skateboarding more safe. And thus by having a patent on it, and enforcing that all skateboards had kicktails that they, that people would . . . not slip off the back of the board when they were doing wheelies.

Author: It's basically a brake.

CS: It's like a brake. And he also invented the double kicktail, which is the basis for the modern skateboard. He made a board where you could take the front kick off and ride it just regular, or you could put the double kick on.

Author: Is that the LX10?

CS: If you measure that board, what's interesting about it is it's a forty-year-old board.

Author: But it's modern.

CS: No, it doesn't really look modern because it looks like a bicycle seat with a piece of wood on it. It looks like a bicycle seat, like one of those Stingray seats.

Author: I remember those boards; we hated them. We called them banana boards.

CS: If you just go to the U.S. Patent Office online, look for Larry Stevenson's patent on skateboarding. You'll see his double kick. My point is that it's about as wide as the skateboards of today. It had a double kick like the skateboards of today. My point is that he somehow knew that that was where it was going to head, and right now those are the only boards besides longboards that you see in the streets. He went all the way to the Supreme Court with this.

Author: Really? How?

CS: His patent was infringed upon by just about everyone. They took it all the way to the Supreme Court, where it was denied to be heard because they deferred to the prior court. He won in some courts, he lost in other courts. They said, "Look, you got the patent, but you didn't mention the Banana Board as prior art."

Author: Well we called the yellow LX10 a banana board, but what do you mean by "Banana Board?"

CS: When someone stands on a skateboard for long enough the ends go up. Simple as that.

Author: But that's not an innovation, that's just wear and tear.

CS: Right. My dad argued, "Do I really have to tell you that a skateboard bends when you stand on it, but the second you take your foot off the middle it straightens out again? This is different than that." So three out of seven courts agreed with him, but they kept going through court to court, appellate courts, and it was the biggest thing, and it went from 1969 to 1979. It took ten years for all this to go down. We were getting phone calls from all over the world. There were people showing up at our door to interview him from France, from Germany, from Sweden, from Japan. This was the father of skateboarding involved in a fight for his life. That's what the whole kicktail thing was.

Author: He patented the kicktail in 1969?

CS: He came up with all the stuff around 1969, and he was awarded the patent in 1971.

Author: Well then that's the biggest innovation during the Dark Ages, I would say. Without the invention of the kicktail there would be no ollies.

The yellow Makaha LX 10 was known as the Banana Board.
Courtesy Rich Novak/Santa Cruz

Charlie's Angels icon Farrah Fawcett gets into the act, riding another 1970s icon – a Logan Earth Ski.

Frank Nasworthy eyeballing an original Cadillac wheel.
Lucia Daniella Griggi

in San Diego that had skateboard composition wheels for sale. My wholesale price for one urethane wheel was probably the same as a set of clay wheels. The person in the store said, "You know, it's never going to work. I mean it's not going to fly." I said okay, whatever. And I ended up just giving a lot of wheels away. I mean not a lot; I probably gave a hundred, or maybe two hundred wheels away.

I lived in Leucadia on Neptune up by Stonesteps and Beacon. I gave the wheels to other surfers and said, "Hey try it out." That inspired word of mouth, and pretty soon people were going to the surf shops and asking for these new wheels.

Author: Off to the races.

FN: Hansen Surfboards had a company called California Surfing Products that repped everything from Aloha Racks to Op swimwear. His salesmen represented the product and it really was very effective. . . . Sales exceeded my ability to finance. I struggled through that—not knowing how to look at it as a business and extrapolate and create a correct budgeting and find the capital to do it.

Author: To quote Bob Seger: "Wish you didn't know now what you didn't know then."

FN: Just to put it in perspective: It was the spring of 1973 when I actually took possession of Cadillac skateboard wheels. Urethane Cadillac skateboard wheels. At that time I went to a bank and I had long hair and everything. They told me, "There's an oil embargo right now and the money's tight and. . . ." I had no idea what a recession was, and we were in a pretty bad recession, really. . . . So I went off and tried to do it myself. And it got around to the point where we were selling hundreds of thousands of wheels. But it was almost a pyramid thing where I would order wheels and sell the wheels I had in order to get the capital to buy the next larger order. It went on like

that for a while until it got big enough that the people working with me demanded more clear financing.

Author: When did you get out of the skateboard business?

FN: I got out when the skateboard park I built in Florida went bankrupt. . . .

Author: You built a skateboard park in Florida?

FN: We went to south Florida to build that, it was in the 1976/77 time frame. There were skateboard parks springing up everywhere. There was a famous park in Carlsbad, and Skatopia I believe was in Anaheim. People were dropping a lot of money to build skateparks, but I didn't have anything close to that. But then we had a chance to go to Florida and get into one of the other larger skate/surf markets, and basically I was a victim of the litigious nature of the sport at that time. I'm not sure what exactly happened, how they do it, but lawmakers can declare a sport inherently dangerous. And once they say that, then no one can sue somebody for breaking a leg skiing, or falling on a snowboard. . . . We built the skateboard park on the premise of a certain amount of liability insurance, but by the time I started construction, that insurance cost increased by six times, which just wiped out that business proposition. I couldn't get enough people through the door to make the proposition work.

Also, I was in Florida in the wintertime searching for a site, going to skateboard parks, skating . . . and everything was neat. Then when I opened in May or April—perfect timing for summer season. School's out! I was in a five-mile radius of five high schools. But it rained every day in the afternoon. I couldn't let people drop into a fifteen-foot-deep pool that's wet, you know. The revenue tapered off because of that, the insurance went up, and so that venture went down the tubes, and that's when I got out of skateboarding.

Gregg Weaver in Huntington Beach, with the same Hobie deck with Cadillac wheels that he was riding back in 1974. During the 1970s, Weaver was the Every Teen, with his bare feet, bushy blonde hairdo, and flowing style on asphalt, in drainage ditches, and in and out of swimming pools. *Lucia Daniella Griggi*

Continued from page 108

The wheels became a huge sensation. Nasworthy's Cadillac Wheels were the first mass-produced urethane skateboard wheels, and almost everything happening today goes back to that light bulb over his head.

The original Cadillac wheels used loose bearings—eight on each side of the wheel. It wasn't until the middle of the 1970s that the next innovation came, when Rich Novak and Jay Shuirman were introduced to sealed, precision bearings by another East Coaster named Tony Roderick.

Urethane wheels allowed skateboarders to go higher, faster, and farther out. Urethane wheels had grip and speed, and the streets, driveways, banked schools, and swimming pools where skaters had been sliding out in the 1960s were now fair game and conquerable.

In California, new terrain was everywhere as an extended drought through the 1970s laid bare drainage ditches, swimming pools, reservoirs, and other terrain that would normally be submerged.

The urethane wheels were fast, but how fast? At places like La Costa, in north San Diego County, the streets were new and the pavement was perfect, and skateboarders gathered day and night with new wheels, new trucks, new boards, and increasingly important and improved safety equipment as they pushed the limits of speed and performance, bombing the hills of Southern California.

For this skateboard boom, the innovation began on the East Coast with Creative Urethanes in Virginia, and later Urethane Casters in New England, but skateboard technology was ignited on the West Coast, from as far south as San Diego and as far north as the Bay Area. In

Continued on page 118

Fourteen-year-old Gregg Weaver weaving around an empty San Marcos pool. According to a *Juice* interview with Steve Olson: "That pool was the perfect eight-foot kidney. It was bitchin'! Bolster was meticulous. I had tile shots, but that's the one he wanted. That was my first cover. I walked into 7-11, saw it, and I was like, 'Hey, that's me!' I only went halfway up. I've heard that my whole life." *Courtesy Surfer Publishing Group*

Gregg Weaver putting a Hobie deck with new Cadillac wheels through its paces, up in the hills of La Costa.
Scan courtesy Barry Haun at the Surfing Heritage Foundation

WE ARE FAMILY

THE LOGANS ON THE ORIGINS OF LOGAN EARTH SKI

There are five Logans: the three brothers, Brian, Brad, and Bruce, their sister Robin, and their mother, Barbara, who was behind the scenes and on the sidelines all through the family's heyday, which began in the late 1950s and hit a peak in the 1970s, when Logan Earth Ski was one of the leaders of the skateboard revolution, as competitors, as manufacturers, and as marketers.

Author: I know Bruce goes as far back as the Anaheim contest in 1965. How far back do you go?

Brian: At least to where we were pulling roller skates apart in the late 1950s. That's when Bruce and I started doing that, 1959.

Author: Where did you get the idea?

Brian: How did we officially start? We started out seeing kids on roller skates and then we got the idea: well, let's take these skates apart and nail them to a board.

Bruce: A group of our neighbors and friends from school all started skateboarding. We were taking our skateboards to school and all got together and then we started a skateboard club.

Author: What were your skateboards like?

LOGAN EARTH SKI*

Bruce Logan

Torger Johnson.

Oak or Birch Wood (non-flexible)
¾″ Thickness—7¼″ Wide   All Steel Chicago Trucks
Regular Size Roller Sports Urethane Wheels
(unless otherwise specified)
ALL SIZE SKATEBOARDS $23.95
To Order Please Check:
- [ ] 25″ Length   [ ] Diamond Tail
- [ ] 29″ Length   [ ] Pin Tail
                      [ ] Rounded Pin Tail
                      [ ] Square Tail

Enclose $23.95 plus $2.00 for postage, handling and sales tax. Mail to **Logan Earth Ski,** P.O. Box 279, Encinitas, CA 92024

Above: An early ad from the first issue of *SkateBoarder* magazine in 1975, laying out the Earth Ski line, equipped with Chicago trucks and Cadillac wheels. *Scan courtesy Surfer Publishing Group*

Below: From left: Brian, Brad, and Bruce Logan, photographed at Brian Logan's home in January 2010. *Lucia Daniella Gnggi*

Bruce: Basically a 2x4. We would nail roller skates to a 2x4. We started out at night.

Brad: That was up on Twenty-fourth Street in Hermosa Beach.

Brian: And then in the early 1960s, we started a skateboard club. I'm only eleven years old, but I was the president, and we've got a dozen kids in our little club. We'd go around doing demonstrations and we would practice at Pier Avenue Junior High every day. At first we were the South Bay Skateboard Club, and then we got a sponsor, Bing Surfboards, so we switched our name over to the Bing Skateboard Team.

Author: Did all of you compete at Anaheim in 1965?

Brian: Yeah, Bruce got second, behind Torger.

Author: Second in freestyle?

Bruce: Freestyle.

Author: You guys competed at Anaheim, and then skateboarding died. But you kept skating.

Bruce: The International Surf Festival ran from 1964 to 1968 in Hermosa Beach. They had Men's Freestyle, Men's Slalom, and the Men's Kick-Turn Race, but other than that there were not any other competitions I was aware of, anyways.

Author: So there were still some things going on.

Brian: Yeah but it just wasn't the same after that Anaheim contest.

Brad: Between 1965 and 1967, Hobie/Vita-Pakt sent teams out

to the schools just to try and keep it going, because I remember they came to our school.

Brian: But very few skateboarders from the 1960s came back into the 1970s.

Author: Your company Logan Earth Ski was a 1970s company?

Brad: That was a pre-planned, meditated move on our part.

Brian: We started our skateboard company in the backyard. We went out to La Costa knowing this magazine was coming out and I was thinking, "Wait until they see Bruce. They're going to blow their minds." Because he had been skating from 1965 and on, and was so far advanced from everybody else going into the early 1970s. We went up to La Costa that first time and people just blew their minds when they saw him.

Brian: La Costa was a big mecca for skateboarding back in the 1970s because you had this community of beautiful hills with brand new, paved black streets and sidewalks, and no houses. We were some of the first to go out there.

Author: Did you guys start up Logan Earth Ski before urethane or after?

Brian: Right before, I think. Yeah it was before, but Bruce was making his own boards under the name of Sunset Skateboards even before we started Logan Earth Ski up in Hermosa Bch.

Bruce: That was late 1969/1970, then 1971 and 1972. It was

basically the twenty-nine-inch diamond board Logan Earth Ski did with my name on it.

Author: How did Logan Earth Ski survive the downturn at the end of the 1970s?

Brian: Why did skateboarding die in 1979? It died for a combination of a couple of reasons. One is there were a lot of injuries at the skateboard parks and the insurance companies were no longer willing to insure the skateboard parks, and the other reason is there were too many manufacturers on the market, and you had some really big people involved in skateboards back then: GrenTec, Free Former, Banzai, and a few others. They had a lot of money and they put a lot of junk out there on the market.

Author: How did it effect you guys in your business? How abrupt?

Brian: When it ended, it ended just like that for everybody. The phones just stopped ringing all at the same time. When it ended, we had to close our factory in Solana Beach and put all the equipment in the garage and storage units, and the next couple of years I didn't know what to do with it all, so I started burning skateboards in the fireplace. Little did I know, thirty-five or forty years later, these boards that cost us ten dollars at the time are worth a few hundred a piece now.

Robin Logan, sister act to the Brothers Logan. A great all-around skater, she was comfortable jumping the limbo stick, popping kick flips at speed, or punching the lip in skateparks. No slouch as a competitor herself, Robin won the women's freestyle division at the 1975 Bahne–Cadillac Championships at Del Mar, and was one of the dominant female competitors through the second half of the 1970s. *Lucia Daniella Griggi*

Kim Cespedes, one of the top female competitors of the 1970s, holding up a pristine Torger Johnson model: "The coolest thing about skating in this era was knowing that all the skate moves we were doing were really fresh. In other words, we were inventing it as we went along. Knowing and seeing new moves for the first time, we were all growing with the sport as it progressed." *Lucia Daniella Griggi*

Bahne formed a partnership with Frank Nasworthy and Cadillac Wheels, and that lead to their co-sponsorship of the Bahne/Cadillac Nationals at Del Mar in September of 1975—the skateboard contest that changed the world.

Author: While researching this book I read a good quote by Sean Cliver: "That's what you get for basing your million-dollar business on the whims of teenagers."

Bill Bahne [BB]: It will always be here. There will always be that core group of skaters and a fringe group doing something different.

Author: I've talked about the business side with Stacy Peralta and Rich Novak and others. The other night I asked Stacy about how much money we were talking about around the time when Steve Rocco and World Industries were going after Powell-Peralta from the 1980s into the 1990s. Stacy said Powell-Peralta was grossing thirty million dollars a year, all through the 1980s. He said one Christmas they sold ninety thousand sets of wheels in a month.

BB: Well we used to do a thousand skateboards a day here. That was peak, around 1974/1975.

The basic Bahne. *Courtesy Todd Huber/Skatelab*

Bill (left) and Bob Bahne, two of the earliest skateboard moguls from the urethane era. *Lucia Daniella Griggi*

Author: I've heard that too. That's amazing.

BB: So I got together with Frank because I heard through the grapevine that he was working on some wheels, so we set it up. And then right after I remember we started running ads in *Surfer* magazine.

Author: What did you think when you saw the wheels? Did you hear angels singing?

BB: Yeah, I saw it right away. Because in the 1960s I skateboarded a lot and I can remember the problems with the composition wheels, hitting specks of gravel and stopping dead in my tracks. We skated the beach walk down in Mission Beach. It was just hell. But the 1970s came around and we had the perfect material for making the skateboards out of . . . and he had the perfect wheel. So we just put everything together at the right time, and boom!

We started off making five skateboards a week, and then twenty, and then fifty, and then a hundred. And when it really caught on, it just jumped. I mean, insanely.

Author: To a thousand boards a day. Were you ready for that, though? Production-wise?

BB: Well . . . it took us a few months to get into it.

Author: How fast did your sales jump from five boards a day to a thousand?

BB: Pretty quick. We had our huge assembly room where we had a bunch of crew who put them all together. We would assemble hundreds of skateboards at a time, because they all went out

A Bahne ad from the inside front cover of *SkateBoarder* volume two, issue one, the first re-issue of the magazine in 1975. *Ad courtesy Surfer Publishing Group*

Bill Bahne. *Lucia Daniella Griggi*

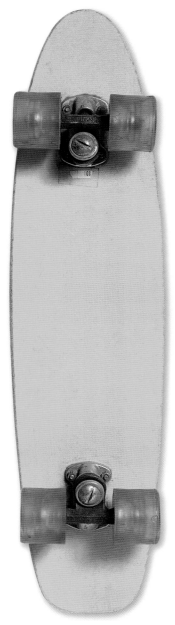

Challenger trucks mounted on a deck.
Courtesy Todd Huber/Skatelab

Challenger trucks mounted on a deck.
Courtesy Todd Huber/Skatelab

Craig Stecyk wrote about Signal Hill in *Built to Grind*. *Rules surrounding the matter were clear and concise. The fastest time on the clock won—no excuses, no worries, and no apologies. All comers were invited, and a number of names in the commercial sector avoided the gig like the plague. Careers and bodies were broken there, and James O'Mahoney, the eminence grise who organized this competition, cut whiners no slack. The diversity of classes at the Hill was unprecedented, and in 1977, skate car and street luge disciplines were included with the regular stand-up classifications.*

In 1977, Santa Cruz Skateboards sponsored the Catalina Classic speed and slalom races, which then moved back to the mainland and became the Capitola Classic. Everyone brought a year's worth of innovation in trucks, wheels, and boards to this race—and things got fast.

In 1976, the first outdoor skatepark of the 1970s was built in Florida. A park at Carlsbad followed soon after, and before long concrete was blooming around the country as skateparks opened by the dozens. Some of the parks were beautifully built; others were shoddy.

During this time, the skateboard protection industry was also evolving, manufacturing helmets, kneepads, wrist braces, and other protection. But just like in the 1960s, kids were still getting hurt at an alarming rate,

Continued on page 132

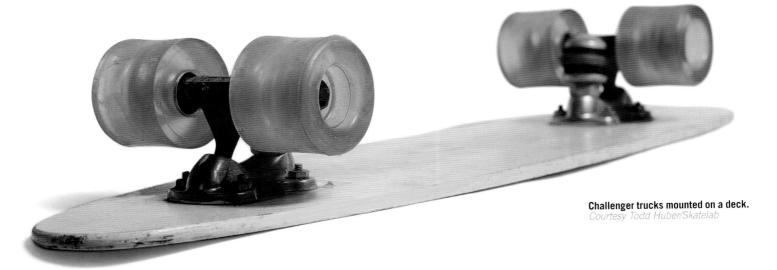

Challenger trucks mounted on a deck.
Courtesy Todd Huber/Skatelab

ORIGINAL SIMS

TOM SIMS EXPLAINS HIS OBSESSION WITH SKATEBOARDING

Author: Where are you from originally?

Tom Sims: I was born in Los Angeles but grew up in New York, New Jersey, and Rhode Island.

Author: What year were you born?

TS: 1950.... In 1960 we took a vacation back to visit my grandparents in Los Angeles—and to go to Disneyland. I saw some kids skateboarding on the sidewalk, and that changed my whole life. I ran into my grandparents' garage and grabbed some ancient metal roller skates, cut them in half, mounted them to a 2x4, took one run and said, "This is it. I love sidewalk surfing...."

It didn't exist on the East Coast and was just starting in L.A. and Southern California.... Skateboarding lead to everything for me: snowboarding, surfing, skimboarding, and wakeboarding. I was living a boarding lifestyle long before the culture was born.

Author: At what point did your fascination and avocation start to become a profession?

TS: I started building four-foot skateboards in the mid-1960s, to simulate surfing. At the time, surfboards were all over nine-feet long, so on those four-foot skateboards I could walk the nose and do kickturns and all that stuff. That went on until the late 1960s, when

A long time ago, in a decade far, far away, in a time called "the seventies," twenty-five-year-old skateboarder Tom Sims was photographed with the Sims Skateboard line in January 1976, at Point Fermin on the Palos Verdes Peninsula. "These were the boards I was selling in surf shops at the time. That same day we shot my first full-color skateboard advertisement, with a girl holding the red Sims Pure Juice wheel in the sun." *Photo courtesy Jim O'Mahoney*

Tom Sims, photographed on his organic avocado ranch along the Santa Barbara coast in June 2009—surrounded by just a fraction of his 40 years of skateboard innovations and archives. *Lucia Daniella Griggi*

The Sims Skateboards team at Paramount Skate Park. Tom couldn't name them all after all these years, but said Tom Inouye is the guy not in uniform, far right.
Photo courtesy Tom Sims

Tom Sims as a stoked grom, circa 1964, when he was already an outlaw, having been arrested for skateboarding the streets of South Jersey—just one way he was ahead of his time.
Photo courtesy Tom Sims

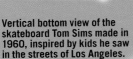

Vertical bottom view of the skateboard Tom Sims made in 1960, inspired by kids he saw in the streets of Los Angeles.
Board courtesy Tom Sims

Horizontal view of the 1960s skateboard that launched a 1970s–1980s empire.
Board courtesy Tom Sims

the shortboard phenomenon hit surfing in Hawaii, Santa Barbara, and Australia. That too changed the world of surfing, and even skateboarding. I started building surfboards in my parents' garage [that] were the first short surfboards on the East Coast. . . . I moved to California in 1971 to find better waves and better skateboard hills. . . . My whole life revolved around skateboarding, surfing, and snowboarding. By the mid1970s, I started building three- and four-foot ash skateboards to sell, and my first dealer was the Channel Islands Surfboards shop. . . .

Author: What were you selling exactly?

TS: Those three- and four-foot wood skateboards and then the thirty-inch fiberglass boards that were like the Bahne boards. I couldn't keep up with the wooden boards, but we could do unlimited fiberglass decks from a company in Burbank called Ampul Corp. I remember going to their factory and smelling all the resin and seeing fiberglass dust fill the air.

Basically the fiberglass boards by Bahne, G&S, Sims, and Santa Cruz were all very similar until Sims started doing the multiple-ply maple boards. My friend—Wee Willy Winkle's

father—had Canada's largest wooded maple door factory in Toronto. Willy, who was a big Sims skateboard fan and champion skateboarder in Canada, called me up and said, "What do you think about laminated maple Sims skateboards?" I jumped on a plane to Toronto and the rest is history.

Author: You couldn't keep up with the wood orders?

TS: I was hiring "Mountain Drivers" (local people from Mountain Drive in Montecito) with band saws to cut them out, and then eventually, in the mid-1970s somewhere, I had to start buying fiberglass skateboard decks from Ampul. We would silk-screen the Sims name and [sell] them as "completes."

I was buying skateboard trucks from some guy in Laguna Beach and then some hardware and stuff from Con Colburn down in Venice. I was buying ACS trucks and Metaflex wheels and eventually ACS and Bennetts. And then finally it was just Gull Wing, Tracker, and Indy. I have all these old price lists and ads that are kind of classic.

I virtually worshiped skateboarding and the whole experience. So basically what happened was from the early 1970s, I was kind of a guru of skateboarding. I mastered the hills of Montecito and the

Tea Bowl—an iconic skateboard reservoir I found a few miles straight up the mountain from the swanky Biltmore Hotel. There was a huge reservoir built by a wealthy woman in the 1920s, but it was now empty, luckily for me and my friends. And I was pretty much the undisputed founder and ruler of the Tea Bowl. I believe there is a scene in the movie *Freewheelin* with Stacy Peralta and I at the Tea Bowl.

By 1977, [Craig] Stecyk and *SkateBoarder* magazine were referring to me as "the Godfather." It was around this time that George Powell called *SkateBoarder* magazine, concerned with all the Sims exposure, and said, "Sims must be paying you bribes." He also said, "Whatever Sims is paying you, I will pay more." Warren Bolster, the editor of *SkateBoarder* magazine, told me this story many times, just laughing out loud hysterically.

During this era, I was driving down to the different contests in SoCal and winning most everything the Sims team and I entered. That all peaked in 1975, when I won the World Skateboarding Championships.

Author: Which event was that?

TS: The Hang Ten World Skateboarding Championship down at the L.A. Arena in September of 1975. When I won there I was on top of the world, then all of a sudden Tony Alva comes along and dethrones me within a very short time. He won the World Championships in a following year, and then all of a sudden Alva skateboards were in huge demand. I had to work hard just to sell skateboards after that, because so many wanted Alva due to his mystique and prowess in empty pools, just as the Dogtown movie depicts him. . . . He was an earthshaking phenomenon. Sims dominated the skateboard mags and then Alva came along and took over, there and in the magazines and the business world.

An interesting thing happened just before this time in skateboard history. Many of the Dogtown skateboarders from the Zephyr team quit Zephyr to join the Sims team when their sponsor got into difficulties. Jay Adams, Bob Biniak, Jim Muir, Paul Constantineau, and Wentzle Ruml all became Sims team riders—most of those guys were using Sims wheels anyway, so when they

TOM SIMS'
QUICKSILVER®

About this ad Tom Sims says, "This was George Powell's first advertisement, and we had a handshake deal that Sims would be his worldwide exclusive distributor. He promised me this enticing deal if I would promote his skateboards and be in his advertisements, and put my endorsement signature on the decks, as Sims was the most prestigious name in the sport at the time." *Ad courtesy Tom Sims*

Thus spake Tom Sims: "The bottom board is one of my first production prototype four-foot skateboards, which I test rode as one of my personal boards in 1972/73. The four-foot skateboards I had made in the mid-1960s were actually rectangular! The top board is one of the first production boards I was building myself to sell to the surf shops. The wheel wells are likely the very first wheel wells ever. The sand and resin textured top was one of the first skateboards with grip, which was the precursor to grip tape." *Boards courtesy Tom Sims*

left Zephyr they came to me [and asked] "Will you sponsor me?" And I was willing to sponsor them—especially Jay and Biniak and the other guys—because they had surfing as their underlying motive for skateboarding. They rode skateboards as if they were surfing and had a style I loved too.

My skateboard team riders were mostly Ventura and Venice-based surfers: Stevie Monahan, Frank Blood, Davey Miller, Richie Vanderwyk, and John Drury and the Venice Rats. Lots of those guys were hot surfers, so it made sense for me to sponsor those Dogtown guys for a while. It felt right, and everything was going great and then . . . Muir busted off to officially form Dogtown Skateboards. I had to say bye to my Santa Monica and Venice crew.

Author: Here is where I get confused, because I seem to think Sims was run by Brad Dorfman and Vision in the 1980s?

TS: By the late 1970s I got very busy getting snowboarding off the ground, and licensed Sims Skateboards to Brad Dorfman in 1981. At the time we had the number-one team with Brad Bowman, Dave Andrecht, Steve Rocco, Todd Swank, Pierre Andre, Chris Strople, Wally Inouye, and a lot of the guys who would become very influential in skateboarding. Many of these guys were the who's who of skateboarding. It's amazing the guys who were on my team and what they went on to do later in life in the board sports world. Pierre Andre started Etnies, and Steve Rocco took over everything, and another name you can put in there is Dave Swift, who became the editor of a big skateboard magazine. Muir formed Dogtown Skateboards, and Todd Swank formed TumYetos. Lamar went on to form Lamar Snowboards.

But at that time, around 1981, I put my focus on snowboarding after Brad Dorfman took over the skateboard license. What's funny in all of this is that just a couple of weeks ago, Brad Dorfman and Dale Smith made a new deal to license Sims skateboards. They are spearheading the licensing of Sims skateboards twenty-five years later.

When I licensed to Dorfman in 1981, there was a recession going on—ninety percent of the skateparks shut down and within eighteen months skate shops were going bankrupt. And that was gnarly to the major skateboard companies, because it wasn't COD back then. The bad debt was overwhelming. Stores could not pay their bills, and hundreds of shops and parks went out of business. That was one of the reasons I licensed to Dorfman. Many of these shops would close down owing us ten thousand dollars or twenty thousand dollars. When Rocco went to COD, that took the risk out of the skateboard industry. He was smart.

Sims made a big surge in the early 1980s, and then we were knocked off the mountain by Powell. Stacy Peralta came on board and built a tremendously strong team and product line with George Powell. He had Steve Caballero and Lance Mountain on the team, and stayed on top sometime into the mid- to late 1980s, until the day Stacy left, and that is the day Powell collapsed. Literally imploded, because Stacy, Rodney, and most of the team bailed. . . . Steve Rocco left Sims and Rodney Mullen left Powell, and they joined to form what would become the biggest skateboard company, World Industries, and Plan B. Rodney and Rocco double handedly changed the sport of skateboarding from vert back to the streets.

A COLLECTION OF SANTA CRUZ BOARDS

The original product from the minds at NHS/Santa Cruz: a pultruded fiberglass skateboard with Sure Grip trucks and Roller Sport Stoker wheels. An order from Hawaii for five hundred lead to another order for five hundred, and then it was off to the races. *Boards courtesy Santa Cruz Skateboards*

After pultruded boards, Santa Cruz went into the woods. *Board courtesy Santa Cruz Skateboards*

A lineup of boards from the earliest days of NHS/Santa Cruz. *Boards courtesy Santa Cruz Skateboards*

Whether or not La Costa was built with Mob money in the late 1960s and early 1970s, the black asphalt and barren streets were definitely enjoyed by this mob—the La Costa Mob, who gathered for a reunion in December 2009. *Ben Marcus*

La Costa high-jumping hijinx made the extra of *Extra* magazine in a photo by Warren Bolster. According to Denis Shufeldt: "The *Extra* photo was Ty Page and Bryan Beardsley. The third guy I can't remember, maybe that was Curt Lindgren. No, it was Mark Bowden. That was the FreeFormer team." *Scan courtesy www.calstreets.com and Surfer Publishing Group*

One of the fastest and most innovative downhill and slalom skateboarders of the 1970s: Denis Shufeldt, photographed in the spring of 2009 at the bottom of Pump Station Hill in San Diego—the scene of many outlaw downhill races, from the 1970s to now. *Lucia Daniella Griggi*

A modern look down one of the many well-paved streets of La Costa. During the 1970s, this was skateboarding's Bonneville Salt Flats, where new urethanes, truck geometries, and skateboard decks were put to the test. *Ben Marcus*

Michael "Smiley" Goldman, one of the fastest men on wheels in the 1970s. Why is he sitting out in the middle of a strawberry field in Watsonville? That road behind him is the infamous Romport Road, which was the inclined drag strip of choice for Goldman, John Hutson, and other NorCal speed demons of the 1970s. From the strawberry fields, they shook up the world. *Lucia Daniella Griggi*

Signal Hill poster.
Courtesy Jim O'Mahoney/ Santa Barbara Surf Museum.

Rocker and roller Terry Nails, guitarist for New Wave band Tommy Tutone, and a dedicated downhill racer, posing with his skates in an ad for *Stroker*, the company that preceded Independent Trucks.

Continued from page 125

and the speed and accessibility of the wheels dialed up the rate and severity of injuries.

In 1976, skateboards also began to get wider. The surfboard-inspired shapes of the past were six to seven inches wide, but new wheels, trucks, and performance demands began to widen boards to over nine inches. The wider boards made a better canvas for graphics, and that colorful side of skateboarding began to blossom, with skater artists like Wes Humpston getting creative with the Dogtown logo and label.

ALL HAIL THE OLLIE

In Florida, a young skater figured out how to make modern skateboards pop off the walls of ramps and pools and into the air—seemingly against the laws of gravity. Alan Gelfand's skateboard move, the ollie, laid the cornerstone for all the radness to come: on sidewalks, in kidney bowls, off ramps, in pools, and onto handrails.

Iain Borden, a British author and skateboard enthusiast, spent countless hours flipping through skateboard magazines, zines, videos, and outside media to write his scholarly, intelligent book *Skateboarding, Space and the City* (2001). In the "Body Space" chapter of his book, Borden discussed the significance of the ollie, and detailed all it inspired in the late 1970s.

In the ollie, the skater performs an aerial without holding onto the board; the maneouver is performed by controlled flight and balance, with a delicate relation between body, board, terrain, and gravitational force. Although it was nearly a year before any other skater could emulate Gelfand's innovation, the ollie soon became the single most important "cornerstone of modern skateboarding," adapted into a bewildering range of variants involving differing directions, rotations, and combinations.

Other technical moves were also developed, including the "invert" aerial (Bobby Valdez, mid-1978), effectively a one-handed handstand; a layback (late 1978), stretching the body off the rear of the board and across the pool wall; and a "rock 'n' roll" (mid-1978), where the skateboard rocks across the top of the wall like a see-saw. Other moves included the "alley oop" aerial, a backside aerial with backwards trajectory (mid-1978); "layback air," a frontside aerial with rear hand grasping the coping and front hand holding the board (Kelly Lind, 1979) and "Miller Flip" (Darryl Miller, 1979); a 360 degree frontside invert aerial where the skater flips over to descend backwards. The "Elguerial" backward invert and fake ollie were inaugurated by Eddie Elguera and Allen Losi respectively.

The difficulty of skateboard moves increased at the same rate as the building of skateparks. Borden states that:

Early, unchallenging skateparks had been built in Kelso, Washington, and in Orange County, California, in 1966, together with a community facility with gently rolling paths in the Ventura County area of Los Angeles [sic] in the 1970s. . . . The first commercial Californian skatepark was the concrete "Carlsbad," opened in the summer of 1975 . . . and by December of 1976 three new parks had been built in Florida—Skatboard [sic] City (Port Orange/Daytona), Paved Wave (Cocoa), and one other at Pensacola—which continued the tradition of surfing already established in pool skating by mimicking Florida's surfing waves in its architecture, varying the steepness of second within one run. Skatboard [that's how they spelled it, apparently] opened one week before Carlsbad, and so lays claim to being the first proper skatepark.

In the first issue of *Skateboarder*, Frank Nasworthy wrote an editorial called "Breakthrough—the Urethane Wheel," in which he explained the past and looked into the future.

Chicago trucks mounted on a deck.
Courtesy Todd Huber/Skatelab

come up with another three dollars for the other two wheels as well, waiting for Con to get more wheels in the shop. Once I had four on… it was sick! Tony Alva says I was the first of the Z-boys to get 'em, but I don't remember. We all loved them the most.

Author: What were the steps to becoming a member of the Zephyr team? Was it because you were a good surfer, or a good skater, or both? Or was it because you had a *Z* in your name?

WR: Ha! Nothing to do with the *Z* in my name. It was pure timing, and I was actually brought to the shop the day after Biniak was put on the team. I went down to the shop and showed up and showed Skip whatever I could do, and I guess it was good enough 'cause I got on!

We all progressed and got better as time went on. Jay, Tony, and Biniak all had "natural talent," but maybe we all did? I think the fact that we skated everywhere was key too. We used skates for transportation, and would only ride the "Big Blue" bus if we were feeling lazy, or going to the north side, Brentwood, or places in West L.A. Everywhere else—we skated. Every overhanging branch, palm leaf, or obstacle became waves. We would get barreled, slash! And rage through town. It was a blast!

Author: Was it a big deal to be on the Zephyr team at first, or did it become a big deal once you guys started dominating skateboard events?

WR: Both . . . being on the team was something to be proud of and we got a reputation really fast! The surf team/P.O.P guys already had a bad rep, so we had to be that way too.

We stood out pretty well wherever we went to compete, and since most of us just thought contests were kooked out [we] just raged and raised hell wherever they were holding contests. We called them "goontests." I remember purposely blowing a final heat at the Long Beach Arena because I didn't want to miss an Aerosmith concert. We didn't really care about winning as much as blowing minds!

Author: What was your specialty as a skater? Freestyle? Pools? Slalom?

WR: Freestyle and surf skate first, pools came later. [I didn't do] slalom until 2003!

Author: Who inspired you as a skateboarder? Which surfers and/or skateboarders?

WR: Skateboarding influences were solely my friends and teammates. Surfers were Gerry Lopez, Rory Russell, Jackie Dunn, Larry Bertlemann, Buttons, Mark Lidell, and local Santa Monica/Venice surfers like John Baum, John McClure, Sarlo, Ho, and all the P.O.P locals: Wayne Saunders, Ronnie Jay, and all the "older" guys who ruled the place!

Wentzle Ruml at Highland Hill in Dogtown, circa 1974/1975. *Sean Valentine, courtesy Wentzle Ruml IV*

Author: Where did you go after the Z-Boys broke up?

WR: Rode for Sims and then others after that. Makaha was my ride out of town in terms of what little touring I did.

Author: Why did the Z-Boys fall apart so soon after the Bahne/Cadillac contest?

WR: Conflict with Ho, Skip, C. R., and Kent Sherwood, [who was] Jay's stepdad and the one who had the molds and glass shop in Venice. I think they had different ideas on what direction Zephyr was to take. There were also some partying issues intertwined through the whole era.

Author: How long did you continue skating? Well into the 1980s? Or were you over it by the end of the 1970s?

WR: I was pretty much done by the end of 1979 or so. It was more important to me to party and get laid than to be true to myself as a skater or surfer. I moved to the East Coast through family intervention—to Cape Cod in March of 1979—and started a new life. I didn't skate again until after the movie was done. Got into racing in 2003 and still do that to this day.

Author: What are you proudest of from that time, and what are your fondest memories?

WR: I'm proud to have been one of the pioneers and to have made up a few moves like the 540-degree slide. To have sort of set the stage for the next generation—and then twenty years later to get a first-place national medal in 2008.

DOGTOWN SKATES

WES HUMPSTON, THE GODFATHER OF SKATEBOARD GRAPHICS

Humpston was a part of the Dogtown skateboard crew beginning in the early 1970s. He wasn't an official Z-boy, but he was skating banks and pools with all of them and was friends with Alva, Adams, Muir, and that crew.

When the Zephyr team began to break up in 1976, Humpston teamed up with Jim Muir to start making Dogtown Skates. Humpston had done hand-drawn art for the Z-boys and other members of the Santa Monica/Venice skateboard crew through the 1970s. But when Humpston began recreating his art on the Dogtown decks, he became one of the pioneers—if not *the* pioneer—and a foundational influence on the thousands of deck graphics to come in the 1980s, the 1990s, and the twenty-first century.

Author: Dogtown is credited with being the first to get really creative with graphics on decks. Do you believe that is true?

Wes Humpston [WH]: Well I don't remember anyone drawing on skateboards or companies doing art on them for each model. . . . I know Craig painted some for the shots in his *Skate* mag articles. I'm not sure when, but I never saw anyone drawing on them like I did.

Author: What came before you as far as deck graphics?

WH: From what I remember they were flat, one-color logos—simple graphics with type. There were some fiberglass boards with the photo/patterns type of thing laminated onto them.

Author: You and Jim Muir started Dogtown Skates, but if I have this correct, he was on the Zephyr team and you weren't?

WH: I wasn't on the Zephyr Skate team, but mid-1970s I skated with most of them on the banks, then the pool. I knew some from school, and others from the beach before DT Skates. I worked at Jeff Ho's shop in the early 1970s, fixing surfboards, doing "leash loops," and even a little art for the shop ad in *Surfer* magazine.

Working at Jeff Ho's was my first job and first year of high school, then skating started up a few years later. . . .

Author: When and where and how did you start skateboarding?

WH: I did some [in the] late 1960s with Kevin Keiser and Craig and Dean Hollingsworth after school on their driveway—making marks by doing cutbacks with the old chalk wheels. Then I started

Wes Humpston began doing hand-drawn graphics on the boards of his Santa Monica/Venice/Z-Boys/Dogtown friends in the 1970s. When he started Dogtown Skates with Jim Muir around 1976, Humpston began reproducing his graphics on decks, which led to the tens of thousands of graphics the world has seen since. This is Wes with two of his contemporary Bulldog skates, photographed in January 2010. *Lucia Daniella Griggi*

An early Dogtown skate, made around 1975 in the backyard. It's 6.5 inches wide by 30 inches long. *Board courtesy Wes Humpston*

full-on in the mid-1970s, when the wheels got better. We would hit a little bank that wrapped around a corner like a wave with local guys after school. . . .

Author: Do you remember what your first skateboards were? Were you drawn to graphics then?

WH: One of my first boards was a twenty-six-inch or twenty-seven-inch I cut out of plywood then put on a shaping stand and tied a cinder block to the middle and fiberglassed it so it would have rocker, like the old Makaha rocker. I had a Z-Flex or two, and I made some from cutting down Muir's Sims longboards.

For the art, in fifth grade I remember cool art in books and Indian headdresses from way back then. We would draw them instead of schoolwork.

Author: What was the original inspiration for the Dogtown Skates logo?

WH: Craig Stecyk. I think I saw it in his photo, spray-painted on a wall. Not sure if Craig had paint on his fingers? Jim and I were making boards for [ourselves] and our friends as things were blowing up. We were driving out to a Val pool with Craig and we told him we were doing Dogtown boards for Dogtown skaters and asked if we

"I rode this 30x8 in early 1977 in the Dog Bowl as boards were getting wider—up to ten inches. The next pool I rode was Gonzo's and I was riding ten-inches and twelve-inches."

Paul Constantineau, original Z-Boy and a rider for Dogtown Skates, photographed in February 2010. He was featured in Dogtown's first ad. *Lucia Daniella Griggi*

could put the cross on 'em, and he said, "Yea!" It was a DTS at first, then I added the skates banner at the bottom and have [now] done ten thousand variations over the years!

Author: At what point did Jim Muir leave the Z-Boys and when did you and Jim start Dogtown?

WH: Not sure the year or month, but Jim, Paul Constantineau, and Bob Biniak rode for Sims for a while after leaving Z-Team. With some of the bigger, longer boards Jim got we cut off the tail and glued it back on, after we grinded it into a wedge to make it a thirty- to thirty-one-inch board. That was what we liked in pools at that time. It seemed like we were always making skateboards when we weren't surfing.

Author: Why did you start Dogtown Skateboards? Was it to make tons of money, or just to do a local project you wanted to do?

WH: It was all about making a better board to ride. The boards really sucked back then, and were flat-out dangerous to ride. There wasn't money in it at the start, but as the boards got better people wanted them and we were turning out a few to ten or fifteen on good weeks, depending on how hard we wanted to work and if there was waves or not. We were selling or trading them for a nice profit so it worked out nice.

Author: When was this around?

WH: We started late 1975 or 1976 I think? It's hard to go by the old photos that show boards in mags 'cause they were months behind what was really going on.

Author: How long did the business last?

WH: Yeah, two years max, until mid- to maybe late 1979, then the wheels started coming off. It was pretty sad. I would hear stories from the guys at Skate City about stacks of our boards at swap meets for five dollars and under a board. Ouch!

Author: Has Dogtown been producing boards since the late 1970s, or has the business come and gone and come again?

WH: Jim has kept Dogtown Skates through the years. By 1979/1980 it was done, so I got a good job in the printing trade, thanks to a girlfriend at the time that was tired of paying for sushi, and did art on the side for a few people. Jim started it back up [in the] early 1980s and I did art for him as side work through the mid-1980s and would sign it as "BDA/Bulldogs Art." I still made boards at home, but was always kind of bitter toward the skate biz. I moved from DT [in the] late 1980s and missed making boards, so I started making them at home again mid-1990s.

From the boyz who brought you skateboarding . . . Skateboards.

Dogtown Skates • The Originals

Paul Constantineau . . . Gettin down at a home town pool.

Paul Constantineau, P. C. Tail Tap Design / 8¼" wide
Jim Muir, Red Dog Design / 9" wide
Wes Humpston, Bulldog Design / 10" wide
Each model available in:
Hotline / 7-ply hardrock maple
Proline / 10-ply
Fibreply / glass and wood

Paul Constantineau, tail tapping at "a hometown pool" in the first ad for Dogtown Skates. Ad courtesy Wes Humpston and Jim Muir

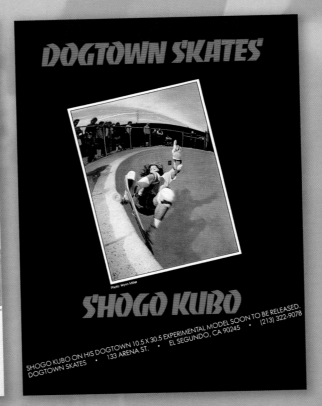

DOGTOWN SKATES

SHOGO KUBO

Photo: Wynn Miller

SHOGO KUBO ON HIS DOGTOWN 10.5 X 30.5 EXPERIMENTAL MODEL SOON TO BE RELEASED.
DOGTOWN SKATES • 133 ARENA ST. • EL SEGUNDO, CA 90245 • (213) 322-9078

Shogo Kubo going big on a board that was 10.5 inches wide and 30.5 inches long. Ad courtesy Wes Humpston/DTS

GONZO'S

THE DOGTOWN BOYS' CHOICE SWIMMING POOL

The Gonzales' swimming pool was located in the quiet Mar Vista neighborhood of West L.A. The pool and property was owned by Mr. Jose Gonzales-Gonzales, an actor who had performed in TV shows from *Bonanza* to *Peter Gunn*. "Mr. G" had a large family and had the pool installed during the pool-building frenzy of the early 1960s by the Anthony Brothers pool company out of South Gate, California.

As the story goes, Ray Flores discovered Gonzo's when he was skating down a street and saw a stream of green water flowing out of an alley. He followed that to a door in a ten-foot-high wall, peeked through, and got a glimpse of Valhalla. Unlike most swimming pools where skaters had to sneak in, Gonzo's was a "permission pool," and so Flores and the Z-Boys skated this perfect pool without fear of arrest or recriminations. And it was at this pool that Tony Alva and the lovely lads pushed the limits of going up and out.

Gonzo's was a huge right-hand kidney. It had a long deep end and a hip you could literally walk up. The transitions were big and mellow, and the entire pool was surrounded with smooth bullnose coping. It was the ideal skating pool.

But as photographer Wynn Miller remembers, "Mr. Gonzales was not always totally cooperative about skating his pool. If you didn't let him know you were coming it could be sketchy—in fact, he heard us in the backyard one afternoon and came running out with a rather large kitchen knife in his hand. Luckily, Ray Flores was there and he mollified him.

"We pretty much lost all of our privileges when we lit the edge of the pool on fire and Tony skated through the flames."

Alva kabob: Here, Tony Alva skates the famous/infamous Gonzo's in the Mar Vista neighborhood of west LA, circa 1977—complete with the contentious ring of fire. In the mid 1970s, Alva was bad, he was *world* wide—one of the first rock star skaters.
Wynn Miller

Tony Alva in the winter of 2010.
Lucia Daniella Griggi

Dogtown Skates Wes Humpston model, circa 1978. According to www.artofskateboarding.com, a mint-condition complete of this model was selling for anywhere from $390 to $999. *Board courtesy G&S*

A 1978 Dogtown Skates Jim Muir model. *Board courtesy G&S*

A 1978 Dogtown Skates Paul Constantineau model. *Board courtesy G&S*

Deck of a 1980 Dogtown Skates Jim Muir Triplane: a transitional board from the late 1970s to the early 1980s, and one of the first boards to use concaves. *Board courtesy G&S*

PLASTICS

151

In *Skateboard Industry News* in October/November 1978, there was a list of skateparks in the United States. There were a total of two hundred skateparks across the country—all built in just over two years. But at the same time, the number of insurance companies willing to insure skateparks was dwindling to one, and getting close to zero.

Just like in the 1960s, skateboarding was imploding as it was exploding, and again it was because of injuries. By the end of the decade, skateboard parks were closing almost before they opened. Companies were folding fast and the boom was busting once again.

Nevertheless, innovation in skateboarding still continued in the late 1970s, even as the boom was beginning to bust. The Powell Corporation introduced their Bones wheels, and Stacy Peralta—a graduate of Dogtown and the Z-boys—teamed up with Powell to form Powell-Peralta, which would become one of the most innovative skateboard companies of the 1980s.

Tracker, Gullwing, Bennett, and a dozen other skateboard truck companies were also turning out new

Continued on page 163

X Caliber trucks on a cambered Sims board.
Courtesy Todd Huber/ Skatelab

COUNTRY ROADS

JACK SMITH ON CROSSING THE COUNTRY ON A SKATEBOARD

Jack Smith is like Forrest Gump combined with the Energizer Bunny. On three separate occasions, Jack has crossed the United States entirely by skateboard. Why did he do it, and do it, and do it again? "First trip in 1976 was done because none of us wanted to have a summer restaurant job," Smith explained. "Went again in 1984 because Gary, Paul, and Bob got tired of hearing my stories about the 1976 ride. I did the trek again in 2003 with Josh Maready, Nick Krest, and Scott Kam to raise research funds and awareness of Lowe Syndrome, which claimed the life of my son Jack Marshall Smith in May of 2003." Below, Smith describes the three trips and some of the boards he rode.

"[In] 1976, the board was a Roller Sports Proline 25x6 inch with RSI trucks and RSI Stoker wheels with precision bearings. [We] began the trip in Lebanon, Oregon, and finished thirty-two days later in Williamsburg, Virginia. My teammates were Jeff French

Jack Smith photographed with his cross-country quiver in the back hills of San Luis Obispo. *Lucia Daniella Griggi*

and Mike Filben. We sent one letter to one potential sponsor, Roller Sports, and they bought it. The deal was all the gear we needed, five hundred dollars to start, five hundred for each of us if we finished. Our support vehicle was a 1969 Firebird. We carried a .22 rifle in the trunk, we had no idea what to expect. . . .

"In 1984, the board was a Madrid Longboard 42x9.5 inch with Tracker trucks and Kryptonics seventy millimeter wheels. The highway between Big Sur and San Simeon was rebuilt in 1983/1984. Just before it reopened in March of 1984, Gary Fluitt, Paul Dunn, and myself skated fifty-six miles of perfect black asphalt on a beautiful day; [we] saw four cars the entire day. It was the best skating day of our lives. By the end of the day, we had decided to make the crossing again.

"Paul wrote a letter to Lee Iacocca asking for vehicle sponsorship. He dug our trip, told us to come pick up a van. Paul, my dad, and I flew to Detroit, where I did a handstand down a corridor in the Walter P. Chrysler World Headquarters building. I traded them a Madrid deck with Indys and Kryptos for keys to a Dodge Ram Wagon van. Didn't sign anything, they just asked when we would bring it back. Times have changed.

"We added Bob Denike to the team, and decided to use the crossing as a fundraiser for the Multiple Sclerosis Society. We started in Newport, Oregon, and finished in Williamsburg, Virginia. Made the crossing in twenty-six days."

"[In] 2003, the board was a RollsRolls 38.5x 9 inch with Independent trucks and ABEC 11 ninety-seven millimeter wheels. This time it was personal: my fourteen-year old son, Jack, [had] died from complications due to Lowe Syndrome on May 6, 2003. I decided to skateboard across the country one more time, in his honor, and to raise research funds and awareness for Lowe Syndrome. It is very rare, only effects boys, [and there are only] about 350 known cases worldwide. The team included Nick Krest, Josh Maready, and Scott Kam.

"This crossing was a huge undertaking, however the Internet made it so much easier to reach out to the industry for sponsorship. The response was incredible, not only from the industry, but also from the worldwide skateboarding community. We were able to raise thousands of dollars for the Lowe Syndrome Association [as well as] awareness of this terrible syndrome. The ride inspired many other skaters around the world to make long-distance rides, many of which raised funds for the Lowe Syndrome Association. My son may be gone, but he is still inspiring skaters and helping to find a cure for Lowe Syndrome. We started in Newport, Oregon, and finished in Williamsburg, Virginia, in a record twenty-one days."

BALMA'S BARN

LARRY BALMA AND THE ORIGIN OF TRACKER TRUCKS

Larry Balma's barn is like the secret Vatican Library of skateboarding lore. Larry himself is a fountain of knowledge: He introduced me to skate people I'd never heard of and kindly gave me access to the vast collection of skateboard magazines and journals carefully hidden away in the massive barn, a collection of all kinds of strange and wondrous things.

Author: What was your first skateboard? What was that like?

Larry Balma [LB]: I started surfing in '58 with a friend whose family had a home in San Clemente. I came home and built a skateboard that week, so I could practice surfing when I couldn't get to the beach. I took a 2x8 and nailed the metal-wheeled skates to that, when everybody else had a 2x4.

Author: You were going wider then already.

LB: The metal wheels would wear out so fast. I'd go around the neighborhood and hustle the ladies, "I'll clean your garage for five dollars." There were always piles of roller skates, so I had an endless supply of trucks and wheels for me and my buddies. And I got paid for them.

Author: When did you buy your first commercial skateboard?

LB: I bought a Hobie skateboard at a Thrifty drugstore. We used to go to the high school dances at the YMCA and sneak in. One night we climbed through an upstairs window and into the equipment room. They had all these roller skates hanging up there, with composite wheels. We'd never seen anything like it before. Look at these wheels!

After high school, I got a job as a lineman and was transferred to Pacific Beach. We skated a little bit, but living in Pacific Beach you could just go surf— all the time. I was a telephone lineman for

Larry Balma offers a quality Tracker truck to the world. *Lucia Daniella Griggi*

about two years and became a commercial fisherman: white sea bass, albacore, and trapped lobster.

I'm patching lobster traps at my house in Leucadia and my friends come by: "Come on we're going skateboarding." And I said "Skateboarding? What are you talking about? I haven't skateboarded for years." And they said, "No, no, we've got these new wheels!" And it was the Cadillac wheel. We went up to La Costa, and that's where it really started for me. I wanted to make a skateboard, so I got some Sure Grip roller skate trucks and built a skateboard and started riding.

The skate crew consisted of Dave Dominy, Dominic Leonard, John Hall, Mike Bing, Craig Dootson, and I. We were discussing the great invention of the polyurethane Cadillac skate wheel and how much the loose ball bearing cone nut setup sucked because the bearings would wear down and they'd spit out. I got out my catalogs and looked up sealed precision ball bearings and prices. I said if we had real bearings we should have wider trucks too.

We talked about making trucks and wheels. I could set up the machining, because I was an engineer on the boats and I looked up how much it cost for bearings. I started figuring out what it would cost to make an axle and this and that and decided that a skateboard would have to cost $30 retail. I said, "Thirty dollars? Nobody would never pay thirty dollars for a skateboard." Meeting over. The idea kind of went away.

A year later I got the same group of guys back together and said, "Hey, Billy Bahne sold a hundred thousand skateboards for $30 a piece last year." Dave Dominy was all over it.

Above: Dave Dominy at home in Cardiff, describing the 1974 origin of Tracker Trucks. *Lucia Daniella Griggi*

We rode all the current skate trucks and evaluated what we liked and disliked about each. I cobbled together some wider trucks and moved the axle geometry around a little bit. Dave Dominy was a far better and more aggressive rider than me; I was the tinker. When we got the right geometry figured out we sat down together with clay and sculpted the look of our truck.

Gary Dodds was a friend from as far back as Cub Scouts; when this was happening he was a pattern maker, living in Cucamonga. He made the master patterns that would ultimately make the molds that the aluminum is poured into at the foundry.

So Dave and I went up to Gary and we had all these skateboards and these prototype trucks. At that point, we had clayed together what would be the look for our truck. And we had some real innovations to it. We established the four-hole mounting pattern. The fixed kingpin. The aircraft hardware. Chromoly axle. I mean at the time, roller skate trucks had case-hardened axles that were soft in the middle and would snap.

Author: You knew that skateboard trucks took a lot more punishment and needed to be much stronger than roller skate trucks.

LB: Our Tracker Fultrack was 4.25 inches wide where a roller skate truck was 1.875 inches wide. We debuted with the Bennett truck that was 2.3125 inches wide and the Bahne truck that was 2.5 inches.

We sold Gary on the idea of building a skate company and formed our partnership: Dodds, Dominy, and Balma. We later incorporated as Tracker Designs, Ltd.

Dave was our skater and the face of Tracker; he would also supervise the shop. Gary was our pattern maker and dealt with the foundry and heat treat. I built the tooling and set up our machine shop. Dave and I shared sourcing of jobbers and materials. Dave and I shared business tasks in the first few months then I took responsibility of legal, accounting, and banking.

We were going into shops with these trucks and they'd say, "Oh no, those are too wide! Your feet will hit the wheels!"

Author: "You'll shoot your eye out, kid!"

LB: We said, "Well, boards are gonna get wider. Look at our boards." And they'd go: "No, no, they're too wide and they won't turn."

And so I got everybody from their areas to rip the Yellow Pages out of all the phone books they had. And the idea was that we would call up the shops: "Do you have Tracker trucks?"

The people at the shops would say, "What are Tracker trucks?"

We'd all say: "Oh, Tracker trucks? You don't have Tracker trucks?"

They'd say: "No, we have Excalibur, we have Sure Grip, we have...."

We'd say: "Oh you don't have Tracker trucks? Okay."

Later! Click.

Author: Clever lad. Isn't that illegal? Whose idea was that?

LB: (Laughing) That was mine.

Author: Oh, you're the same guy who got little old ladies to pay you for taking those roller skates out of their garages.

LB: Yeah, you bet.

The Tracker crew, circa 1978. Dave Dominy is third from the right in the back row. Larry Balma is second from the left. *Courtesy Larry Balma*

Above: A Tracker trucks ad, featuring one of Tracker's founders, Dave Dominy.

Right: A Tracker ad, circa 1989, looking back on fifteen years of skateboard truck evolution. *Ad courtesy Larry and Louise Balma*

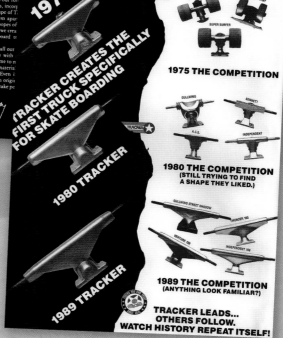

BALMA'S BARN

The Balmas have been in the skateboard business since 1975, and they've saved many, many things from Tracker Trucks and TransWorld Publishing, which Larry founded in the 1980s. *Lucia Daniella Griggi*

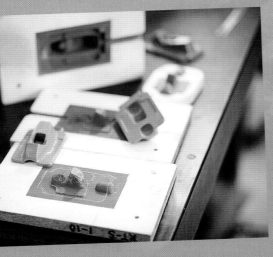

Larry is a tinkerer and is always experimenting, whether it's with magnesium trucks or a new profile. Here he is painting a master pattern for a new truck baseplate prior to making the mold. Note the Lamborghini Miura under the cloth cover. *Lucia Daniella Griggi*

With all the tools he has, you could probably build an aircraft carrier in Larry Balma's machine shop, but Larry works smaller than that. Here he is grinding cold rolled steel to make a jig fixture. *Lucia Daniella Griggi*

This is how skateboard trucks are modeled before they are molded: "He took a hundred grams of clay. . . ." *Lucia Daniella Griggi*

The deck of an original Zephyr skateboard, formulated by Jay Adams' stepfather Kent Sherwood, who worked for Dave Sweet Surfboards. *Board courtesy Jeff Ho*

The bottom of an original Zephyr skateboard. *Board courtesy Jeff Ho*

An E/Z Ryder skateboard, developed by Kent Sherwood and ridden by Jay Adams and others, after the breakup of the Zephyr team. *Board courtesy Ray Flores*

Z-flex board. *Board courtesy Ray Flores*

SERIOUS IMPRESSIONS

SKITCH HITCHCOCK AND THE ORANGE COUNTY SURFER–SKATER CREW

About halfway between the Dogtown guys up north in L.A. and the La Costa guys down south in San Diego County, Skitch Hitchcock was part of an Orange County surf/skate crew who claimed Salt Creek—near Dana Point—as their home grounds, and made a serious impression on freestyle, slalom, and speed skateboarding in the 1970s. In a 2009 article by Vickie Chang in *The OC Register*, Herbie Fletcher remembered this crew: "They'd skate everywhere around Dana Point. And they worked at it. Every sunrise, they'd be down at Salt Creek surfing. And then it'd blow out, and they'd skateboard all day—like all day. Skitch was good. He was one of the guys leading the pack."

Hitchcock and his brother, Garrison, were originally from Long Beach, but gravitated south to the better waves of the OC in the middle of the 1970s. When the urethane revolution hit, Hitchcock joined the Hobie team, and along with Garrison, Mike Weed, and Dale Smith, the Salt Creek/Hobie guys began to make a name for themselves in everything from freestyle to Signal Hill.

As Russ Howell said: "I was introduced to Skitch Hitchcock at the 1975 Bahne/Cadillac Del Mar Nationals. He rode with a very similar style to my own and we placed First and Second as Hobie Team Riders in the Senior Freestyle Division. Skitch was more than just a skateboard rider, he was innovative and very talented at fabricating skate products. He designed skateboards, ramps, and unique roller devices that were always a welcome diversion from the normal way of doing things. Skitch was never financially rewarded for his contributions to the sport and it was obvious that he rode because he truly loved skateboarding. Skitch remains one of my favorite skaters and one of the sport's greatest contributors."

Skitch Hitchcock.
Lucia Daniella Griggi

Above: Jeff Ho standing in front of Horizons West Surf Shop in the summer of 2009. What began as Jeff Ho Surfboards and Zephyr Productions in 1971 became Horizons West Surf Shop in 1977, when Ho moved to Hawaii and Nathan Pratt took over the business. Immortalized in the *Dogtown and Z-Boys* documentary and *Lords of Dogtown*, the building was designated a Santa Monica city landmark in 2007. Sadly, Horizons West became a victim of the internet and the economic downturn in July 2010. *Lucia Daniella Griggi*

Right: A Zephyr ad circa 1975, from *SkateBoarder* volume two, issue one. *Scan courtesy Surfer Publishing Group*

corralling kids behind chain-link fencing, watch out, 'cause it's due for a downturn. Sure enough, after its peak following the Newark Hester contest, the biz took a sliding dump.

By February 1979, skateparks had multiplied like fertile rabbits, topping off at about 400 facilities across the U.S. Most couldn't survive however: bad design, injury litigation, and kids unwilling to "pay to play" took their toll, and the parks began closing as quickly as they had opened. They started out as the "future of skateboarding" and ended under the blade of the bulldozer.

Jerry "Taters" Hurtado, the manager of the Big O Skatepark at the time, remembers:

Jeff Ho's 1960s Paul Revere
special, before urethane.
Board courtesy Jeff Ho

Profile of an original OZ Zephyr, the choice
of the Z-boys when they shook up the world.
Board courtesy Jeff Ho

*Every parent of a kid with a broken femur or wrist wanted to
grab a lawyer and sue for the one-mil cashout. Plus, most of the park
designs were crap. Guys who had never stepped on a board or even
cared were laying cement.*

*Still, the super-talented skaters kept improving and pulling ahead
of those less skilled in the process; you either kept up were forced to
sit down and watch. Kids were over it. By the beginning of the '80s,
existing skateparks had dwindled to less than a dozen.*

Different people point to different events as the
terminus of skateboarding's second wave of popularity,
but most will agree that it was the decision in 1980 to
close *SkateBoarder* magazine and turn it into *Action
Now*—and include skateboarding with BMX, inline
skating, and other sports. That was the beginning of the
end of skateboarding's second boom. Skateboarding had
exploded in a blaze of innovation, money, successes,

Above: Brite Lite incomplete.
Courtesy Cris Dawson

A Ray "Bones" Rodriguez Brite Lite.
Courtesy Cris Dawson

Bottom of a yellow Beamer.
Courtesy Cris Dawson

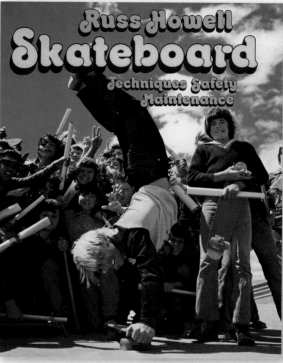

Skateboard superstar Russ Howell shows how to do his famed handstand on the cover of his 1975 book, *Skateboard: Techniques Safety Maintenance.*

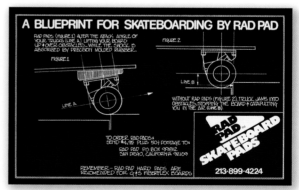

Rad Pads were to skateboards what lifters are to four-wheel-drive trucks: clearance and turning for increasingly sophisticated terrain. *Ad courtesy www.calstreets.com*

A transitional figure from the surf-style of the 1970s into the skater-punk style of the 1980s, Steve Olson is still styling.
Lucia Daniella Griggi

Backside or frontside, Rick Blackhart ruling the fifteen-foot full pipe at the Cunningham Lake skatepark on a rainy day in San Jose in January 2010.
Lucia Daniella Griggi

Above: Rick Blackhart was another transitional figure from the 1970s to the 1980s. Born a rebel in San Jose, Blackhart was kicked out of high school for skateboarding through the rafters of the gym during a rally. And that was how it went. Blackhart was not from the surf-skate school: "I hated surfing," Blackhart told *Juice Magazine*. "I hated that Fluid Floyd Aquanoid crap. I lived in Santa Cruz for five years, and I think I got in the water twice. Once was just to walk along the beach in a wetsuit with a surfboard to pick up chicks." Blackhart traveled south, skated places like Upland, and saw the light at the end of the fullpipe. Back in San Jose, Blackhart was one of the skaters who pushed the R&D of Independent Trucks and lead the NorCal skate revolution. *Lucia Daniella Griggi*

Left: Steve Olson in an ad for Independent Trucks that is considered one note in the *Thus Spake Zarathustra* of the street-skating revolution.

Free On The Streets

London skater Dennis Coghill disrupts the balance of the world.
Evening Standard/Getty Images

UP AND OUT

SKATEBOARDING MOVES AWAY FROM SIDEWALK SURFING AND INTO THE AIR: 1981–1991

Poster for the 1987 feature film *Thrashin'*.

The 1980s are when sidewalk surfing became less about surfing and more about sidewalks—when skateboarding moved away from its origins in the sunny surf and found increasing popularity in the shady turf.

Most skate historians agree that skateboarding climbed out of the concrete rubble created by the destruction of hundreds of skateboard parks in the 1970s and began to rise again when *Thrasher* magazine began publishing in 1981.

The closure of most of the skateboard parks in the United States forced skateboarders to get creative— make their own parks, experiment with new terrain. As Michael Brooke wrote in *Concrete Wave*:

In the '80s the plywood ramp and streetstyle revitalized skateboarding just as the urethane wheel had revitalized the sport in the '70s. Forced to take an underground, do-it-yourself attitude, skaters began to create their own wooden skate ramps in backyards and empty lots and turn previously unrideable street terrain, such as walls and handrails, into free-skateparks. Skater-owned companies became the norm and innovations in board and truck size allowed the trick envelope to be pushed even further.

A little bit Bogart, a little bit Brando, all topped with heaps of attitude: Duane Peters now was Duane Peters then. A troubled kid, Peters was banished from Newport Beach to Michigan for a year. He came back in the 1970s when the second skate boom was hitting, and he made himself a skateboard out of a 2x4 and roller-skate wheels. Toward the end of the 1970s, Peters was Power Punk for Now People, starting up in the late 1970s as a rider for Dogtown Skates, then Santa Cruz. Peters took punk into the pools and bowls and innovated a set list of moves: acid drop, layback grind, Indy air, sweeper, backside layback grind revert, the invert revert, fakie thruster, and the fakie hang-up, also known as the Disaster, which gave Peters his nickname: Master of Disaster. Peters has played with numerous punk bands, struggled with heroin, and lost a child to a car accident. Good times, bad times, Peters has seen more than his share of both. *Lucia Daniella Griggi*

GOING PUNK

In the 1980s, skate style pulled away from surf style and began to follow other styles, and then take the lead. Coming out of the groovy disco 1970s, the world rebelled by going punk and New Wave, and a section of skateboarding adopted that style as skate style. The style changed from the bushy hairdos of the 1970s—cotton trunks and striped shirts—to striped faces, Mohawks, and leather jackets.

Many historians point to Steve Olson as the guy who brought skate and punk together, and it was the San Francisco scene that turned him. Olson was a SoCal kid who went north to hang with the NorCal guys at Santa Cruz/NHS, Ermico, and Independent. This was a time when the NorCal/SoCal rivalry was strong. As Big O Skatepark owner Jerry Hurtado said in "The Crash, the Revolution, and Going Underground," by Bob Denike writing in *Built to Grind*: "Olson was like a stepchild back then, when there weren't too many punkers around. He was the chap at the time, a major influence who inadvertently turned the skate world on to punk. I

Santa Cruz Skateboards 1983 Duane Peters Pro model.
Board courtesy G&S

Skull Skates 1989 Duane Peters Tub Tech Concave.
Board courtesy G&S

Variflex 1985 Allen Losi.
Courtesy Todd Huber/Skatelab

RAMPING UP

The Hawk family and the NSA represented the "Ozzie and Harriet" side of skateboard competition, but there were other options for skaters who wanted to compete, but not necessarily behind fences.

In 1983, the first "street-style" skateboard contest was held in San Francisco's Golden Gate Park, and it was won by local skater Tommy Guerrero. Street-style skating was "sidewalk surfing" with more of an emphasis on "sidewalk" than "surfing." Rising stars like Guerrero, Natas Kaupus, and Mark Gonzales were pushing the limits of street skating—pushing down the sidewalk, or out in the street, and making use of whatever terrain presented itself: bus chairs, concrete walls, curbs, hobos, cops, Mercedes, fire hydrants. Whatever, the point of true, core street skating was to react to whatever presented itself—and in that way, it was returning to the roots of surfing while moving away from the surf-skate influence of the 1970s.

The first "Ramp Jam" was also held in 1983, on a private ramp in the backyard of Joe Lopes, a NorCal skater with cool parents who lived in San Leandro. Video of that event shows that a San Jose kid named Steve Caballero was clearly smoother and higher than everyone else. Caballero would later emerge as one of the biggest skate stars of the 1980s.

According to Iain Borden in *Skateboarding, Space and the City*:
From 1977 onward, skateparks were also increasingly complemented by the provision, often by skaters themselves, of ramps. At first such ramps were seen as a way of providing vertical terrain for those who were without access to skateparks or Californian pools, and by 1980 the Rampage company had already sold 4,000 sets of ramp design blueprints across America as well as to 45 other countries. Following these early ramp constructions, when many skateparks closed in the early 1980s, ramps became the staple terrain for skaters, and greatly contributed to skateboarding's resurgence in the mid-1980s.

The answer to these blues lies close at hand, at the end of a hammer and a saw. The answer is ramps.

In 1981, Action Now *(formerly* SkateBoarder*) gave information on ramp construction, and the then new magazine* Thrasher *did likewise, with a 1983 issue giving detailed ramp plans quickly becoming sold out. By the 1990s ramp plans were readily available off the Internet.*

Backyard ramps became the rage, as all it took was some solid woodworking skills and a vacant lot or understanding parents, and any skater could have their own park.

Neil Blender is another 1980s icon who has a move named after him: the Lien Air is a frontside air grabbing the nose or heel edge with your front hand. "Lien" is "Neil" spelled backwards, so he qualifies. Lien—sorry, Neil—did the art for this G&S 1987 Neil Blender "Coffee Break" model. *Board courtesy G&S*

Eighties skaters had surf style, punk style, and some had Lowrider style. Doug "Pineapple" Saladino was one of the leaders of that "street" *escuela*, scoring a two-page interview in the July 1980 issue of *Lowrider* magazine—with Cheech and Chong on the cover. Born and raised in San Diego, Saladino began competing at the age of 11, at the 1975 Bahne–Cadillac championships in Del Mar. He won his first contest when he was fourteen. Saladino was one of the few freestylers who made the shift to pool and bowl riding, becoming one of the top competitors in both freestyle and vert in the 1980s. "I started out with freestyle and slalom," Saladino says. "As pools came around and became more prevalent, I transitioned successfully . . . not too many of us were able to do that." *Lucia Daniella Griggi*

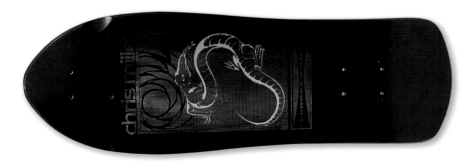

G&S 1984 Chris Miller "Mini Lizard."
Board courtesy G&S

remember seeing him go from surf rat to punk rat, with a leather jacket and checkerboard flat top."

South San Francisco is the Industrial City—you can see that written on the side of a mountain as you drive in from the south—and it was this part of the world that diverted the skateboard industry away from the ocean and onto the streets. According to *Built to Grind*:

The combination of punk rock and street skating bred a different type of skater; a guy who didn't need the norm, didn't need the rules and restrictions, didn't need the equipment and the lifetime park pass. All he needed was his leather jacket, his 501s, his Chuck Taylors, and a street skate. It could have been a marketing move, but at the same time, it was inevitable. You had to go back to whatever was there before.

In February 1980, Olson was featured in what is considered the first "street skating" ad for Santa Cruz Skateboards in *SkateBoarder*, under the tagline "Free on the Streets."

Tony Hawk had been a frustrated, hyperactive child who drove his parents crazy up until the age of nine—when his brother Steve handed down a blue Bahne skateboard with Cadillac wheels: "When he started getting good at skating it changed his personality," his brother Steve says on Tony's official website.

"Finally he was doing something that he was satisfied with. He became a different guy; he was calm, he started thinking about other people and became more generous. He wasn't so worried about losing at other things—he wasn't as competitive at Pac Man as he had been." To which his mom Nancy added: "I was just glad he was taking all his energy out on skateboarding and not on me.

Continued on page 200

Above: Hosoi 1987 Christian Hosoi Street Flag. Hosoi grew up skating with and inspired by the greats of the 1970s: Shogo Kubo, Jay Adams, Tony Alva, and Stacy Peralta. He took that Dogtown attitude and "anything is possible" style into the 1980s.
Board courtesy Todd Huber/the Skatelab

Hosoi quiver from left: Hosoi 1987 Christian Hosoi "Vert Flag," Hosoi 1988 Christian Hosoi "Hammerhead Collage," Hosoi 1989 "Irie Eye" team deck, and Hosoi 1986 Hammerhead. *Boards courtesy the Board Room/Santa Cruz*

Street skating took a backseat to vert and even freestyle in the first Bones Brigade video, which was released in 1984. The Bones Brigade videos were the brainchild of Stacy Peralta and Craig Stecyk, who turned their communication skills toward skateboarding when Peralta and George Powell got hyphenated and created their skateboard brand in 1978.

Powell was the engineer, while Peralta was the buzz-maker and marketeer—and a genius for finding unknown talent that was about to bloom: Rodney Mullen, Tony Hawk, Tommy Guerrero, Steve Caballero.

Peralta formed the Powell-Peralta team and, beginning in the late 1970s, shot the riders using Super 8 and three-quarter-inch Beta Cam. In 1984, Peralta and Stecyk edited together the best footage of Powell-Peralta team riders and put out the *Bones Brigade Video Show*. As Peralta relates in the narration to the special edition of the DVD, these videos were available before commercial VHS machines were easily accessible to the public. But once the world began buying and/or stealing their own VHS players, they could study Rodney Mullen's "modern freestyle" antics, like the flatland ollie, the ollie flip, and a hundred other completely unique tricks that sometimes came too fast to name. The *Bones Bridge Video Show* also featured a young, skinny, seemingly frail Tony Hawk flying through the air with the greatest of ease out of pools and bowls; slow-motion shots detailed the incredibleness of his airwalks and finger flips.

The media competition between *Thrasher* and *TransWorld* and the ever-increasing number of skate zines popping up around the country was heightened by the emergence of video. Moves caught in single frames or sequences could be studied, but not really understood. Video could be watched over and over and over again, and the best skaters from the best companies became superheroes as they spread the cutting-edge to the grateful masses—who could now study the tricks the best skaters did, and replicate them.

Vertical skating on ramps and bowls were featured in the original *Bones Bridge Video Show*, linked together by Lance Mountain laying down the foundation of street skating—sidewalk surfing plus—as he bombed the streets of Los Angeles, carving grass, embankments, curbs, walls, drunks, and whatever man or nature put in his way.

The *Bones Bridge Video Show* also featured the ramp and bowl skating of Mike McGill, Steve Caballero, and others, and the rest of the world was amazed: "There had been no outlet to see this kind of skateboarding," Stacy Peralta says in the voiceover. "Magazines didn't do it justice, and so when the Bones Brigade videos came out, I think it helped to revitalize an industry that was all but dead at the end of the 1970s and into the early 1980s."

In the early 1980s, Mike McGill unleashed a vert trick that is considered by many to be the jumping-off point for a new era in vertical skating. Borden described the progression in *Skateboarding, Space and the City*, beginning with an awed description of the McTwist by Jocko Eyland in "Epiphany at Mecca," from the July 1997 issue of *Thrasher*.

As he flew out 4 or 5 feet, he went upside down and spun. And kept spinning . . . until he had turned 540°, completely inverted at the 360° point with his head 3 feet above the coping. . . . In that moment when he was flying with his top and bottom reversed, everyone who was watching the pool saw something so amazing as to be unbelievable. . . . Things had changed. In an instant a new dimension had opened up.

This was a move which heralded a new era again in vertical skating.

By the end of the 1980s, Tony Hawk was doing varial, ollie and flip variations of the 540, and skaters generally were performing even more complicated variations of the combinatorial moves. In particular, by 1988 they began to refocus on the top edge of the wall (rather than just the air above it), including the Jetton grind (frontside grind to revert), cess-slide 50-50s and other such lip tricks as the "due process" fakie ollie to frontside nosepick, with back truck on deck, followed by frontside aerial to re-enter (Joe Johnson, 1988), fakie ollie 180° nose-taps (Tony Hawk, 1989), and the ollie to front truck grind (Bod Boyle, 1989). These were "balance point" tricks, where the skater controls the lip with both body and board—through this process, the skater could think of their body and terrain beneath as one entity. Alternatively, skaters were spending a longer time in the air through ever more complex body-board spatial productions; by 1991, skaters such as Danny Way were also experimenting with 900° (2.5 full rotations) aerials. By the same date, skaters were also undertaking many moves backwards, or switch-stance.

These extremely technical and dangerous moves (many performed at eight feet or more above the ground) were partly

Keith Meek, at the newly reconstituted Buena Vista pool, in the backwoods of Watsonville. "I was a vert skater in the 1970s more than I was in the 1980s. More known for my backyard pool skating than anything, not really ramps." *Lucia Daniella Griggi*

Sean Cliver did the art for this Powell–Peralta 1990 Bucky Lasek "Lasek Stadium" deck. *Board courtesy Todd Huber/the Skatelab*

Jeff Grosso. *Lucia Daniella Griggi*

When Lance Mountain did the art for his Powell–Peralta 1989 "Junior" model, he couldn't have known in 1989 that his son, Lance Ronald Cyril Mountain, would fill Senior's footsteps as a hot skater his ownself. *Board courtesy James Lang*

Jason Jesse. *Lucia Daniella Griggi*

Representing Ohio: Rob Roskopp in black and white with the original series of Jim Phillips monster graphics, the first series graphic applied to a skateboard. *Lucia Daniella Griggi*

A Santa Cruz 1987 Jeff Grosso with art by Jim Phillips. Santa Cruz released a cavalcade of great decks in the 1980s, courtesy of legendary artist Jim Phillips. One of his first designs to hit the punk market dead-on was the Steve Olson model, featuring the bold Dot logo and black-and-white checkerboard motif; when it comes to vintage boards, this one makes even the most hardened punk swoon. In the mid-1980s, Phillips let some illustrative steam loose at NHS with Rob Roskopp's first pro model, which to this day remains a testament to clean, iconic, and well-executed graphics. The subsequent four models in the Roskopp Target series have driven collectors nuts over the years, and I know of only one to complete the set in mint condition. Perhaps the most commonly coveted of the Santa Cruz boards is the Jeff Grosso Wonderland. Maybe it's the Disney thing, maybe it's the drug thing, but whatever it is, it made some guy drop $2,700 on one, and there remain a bunch more lined up to score this deck. *Boards courtesy the Board Room/Santa Cruz*

Santa Cruz Jeff Grosso decks, including at right, a 1988 "Jeff Grosso is the Real Thing!" *Board courtesy the Board Room/Santa Cruz*

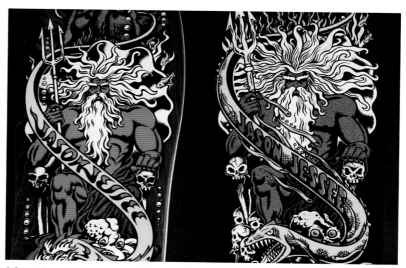

A Santa Cruz 1988 Jason Jesse "Neptune Shark," with art by Jim Phillips (left), next to a 1989 Jason Jesse "Neptune Mermaid". *Boards courtesy the Board Room/Santa Cruz*

Rick "Spidey" Demontrond was a 1980s skater who had a segment in Santa Cruz' *Streets of Fire*, and "was known for his backyard ramp and huge skate sessions," according to www.artofskateboarding.com. Santa Cruz 1987 Rick Demontrond "Spidey" model. *Board courtesy James Lang*

Santa Cruz Skateboards 1988 Jason Jesse "Sun God" model, although according to www.artofskateboarding.com, "Technically, this graphic is actually a close-up of Neptune's face from Jason's other 'Neptune' model. I guess making the face orange, yellow and red tones made it more 'sun-like.' *Board courtesy James Lang*

Texas/New York/NorCal artist Johnny Mojo did the graphic on this Santa Cruz Skateboards 1991 Jason Jesse "Jesse Guadalupe" model. *Board courtesy James Lang*

Snakes, heathens, and a half-naked wild woman in a crockpot. Paging Dr. Freud! Art by Jim Phillips for a Santa Cruz Skateboards 1989 Steve Alba "SC Salba Voodoo." *Board courtesy James Lang*

Santa Cruz 1989 Eric Dressen "Celtic Rose." Art by Kevin Marburg. *Board courtesy James Lang*

Steve Olson Skates 1984 "Steve Olson SOS Model." *Board courtesy James Lang*

H-Street and Osiris founder Tony Magnusson. The missing fingers were part of the partnership ritual that all founders of H-Street went through. (Just kidding. There's a story behind the missing digits–ask Tony.) Magnusson's originally from Sweden. Inspired by other Swedish skaters, he left Sweden at sixteen years old, stowing away on a Viking longboat and hopping icebergs from Sweden to America. His first sponsor in America was a small San Diego company called Uncle Wiggley. The company was so small that it couldn't really afford to support the rising skateboarder and T-Mag joined the company as an owner, learning all the basics of business and manufacturing. In 1986, Magnusson and his partner Mike Ternasky co-founded H-Street, which many consider the father of the skater-owned companies to come. After Ternasky died in a car accident in 1993, T-Mag went on to found Osiris Shoes. Still a top competitor, he owned the Legends of Skateboard World Championships in Germany from 2001 to 2005 and is also a multi-champion of the Soul Bowl (masters) in Huntington Beach, California. *Lucia Daniella Griggi*

A Santa Cruz 1980 Salba Bevel. According to www.salbaland. com, "[T]he Santa Cruz team of Steve Olson, Steve Alba, and later Duane Peters brought the new culture of punk rock to the forefront of skateboarding. . . . In 1979 Santa Cruz introduced the Steve Alba Bevel model. The Salba Bevel featured the first deep side-to-side concave and upturned nose to ensure foot placement during radical maneuvers." *Board courtesy Santa Cruz Skateboards*

THE DRAGON

STEVE CABALLERO AND THE CABALLERIAL

Steve "Cab" Caballero is a classic case of a skatepark kid made good. Born in 1964—the Year of the Dragon—Caballero utilized the dragon theme in his graphics, as he became one of the leading skateboard stars out of the 1970s and into the 1980s. He started off riding BMX, inspired by Evel Knievel—a major cult hero of the 1970s. He began skateboarding at twelve, just goofing around—when just making the turn from the driveway to the sidewalk was a big deal. A big fan of comic books and monster magazines, skateboard magazines also caught Caballero's fancy and inspired a deeper interest—beyond the driveway.

Caballero became a teenager just as skateparks were sprouting up around the world. His first experience was at Concrete Wave Skatepark in Anaheim—during trips with dad to Disneyland. Closer to home, Caballero became a regular at the Winchester Skate Park in San Jose and then bailed on Winchester for the Campbell Skate Park— because it was only $1 a day to skate. Caballero competed with the Campbell Skate Park team. He had a natural talent and a driven enthusiasm—because skateboarding was something where a little big man could excel.

Stacy Peralta saw that excellence early on, and Caballero became one of the first team members for Powell Peralta in 1978—at the age of fourteen. By 1980, Caballero was already a veteran of skatepark bowl competitions and he had christened his own trick: The Caballerial,

The many faces of Steve "Cab" Caballero and friends. This portrait was taken in the winter of 2010 at Caballero's home in Campbell, California, where he lives surrounded by comic books and superheroes with his wife Rachel, daughter Kayla, revved-up son Caleb, and two protective dogs. *Lucia Daniella Griggi*

aka a fakie 360 ollie. The Half Cab is a fakie 180 ollie.

Into the 1980s, Caballero was one of the star members of the Bones Brigade, featured in the series of action sports videos produced by Stacy Peralta and Craig Stecyk for Powell-Peralta. Steve Caballero was one of the major skateboard stars of the 1980s, and he surprised himself and his parents by earning a very good living with board sales and shoe sales. One of his better qualities is that he is very loyal to the companies who first sponsored him. Thirty years later, he is still with Vans and Powell—Peralta.

The sales of this Powell–Peralta Steve Caballero "Dragon Pig" shocked Caballero—and his parents—as he transitioned from 1970s BMX/ skatepark rat to 1980s superstar. *Board courtesy G&S*

Powell–Peralta 1989 Steve Caballero "Full Dragon" model, with art by Sean Cliver. *Courtesy James Lang*

"MACKT-WEEST!"

MIKE MCGILL AND THE MCTWIST

Born in 1964, it was twenty years later that Mike McGill was at the end of a long skateboard session in Sweden, when he did something no one had done before: A 540 rotation—one and a half times around. He worked on it in Sweden, added a flip to the rotation and started a revolution: "'It just felt better and looked better," McGill was quoted in *The Origin of the McTwist* on skateboardingmagazine.com. "Teammate Rodney Mullen called it the McTwist. The name has stuck ever since. Since then, the move has become almost a requirement for skateboarders and snowboarders to be able to compete at the highest level. 'After I did the McTwist in competitions, you had to do it to qualify and a lot of guys didn't like me for that,' McGill said laughing."

McGill increased his legend as a teammate of Steve Caballero, Lance Mountain, and the Bones Brigade team, starring in all of the Powell-Peralta movies produced by Peralta and Stecyk.

Asking around for some comment on McGill, Jim Fitzpatrick provided a taste of what it was like to be around the inventor of one of the transitional skateboard moves of the 1980s:

"Skateboarding around the world with Mike, at demos and other events, was always an amazing experience. He was a professional. He was a really dedicated skater, and capable of cranking up his ability for each 'show.' Especially in Europe, in '88 and '89, there would be a frenzy when he dropped in on vert ramps: 'Mack-Tweest! Mack-Tweeest! Mack-Tweest!' Kids had to see it to believe it. Mike was humble, and it sort of embarrassed him, but he was proud too, and he never disappointed. He'd drop in and pull a few backside airs and then, 'Whooop!' There it was! The McTwist right before their eyes, and the crowd would just go nuts!

"The kids would glance at their friends, 'Did he? Yeah he did!' In 1988 we did a nighttime show in Zurich in a soccer stadium. 8,000 kids crammed into the stadium with a 48-foot wide vert ramp on a stage set up at one goal line, with BMXers and inline skaters, a Monster Costume contest, a bikini contest, and a Battle of the Bands, all going on before the Bones Brigade took the stage on the vert ramp. I was walking around thinking, 'What the hell is this, show business?' Then some guy grabbed at me, 'Are dey raydee?' as a deep DJ-voiced announcer started introducing the 'BONESSSSSS BREE-GAAAAAAAAAAAYDE' with all the special effects and the names all stretched out, 'Steeeeeeeeeeeeve Caballerrrrrrrrrrrrrrrro!

Mike McGill, photographed in front of his skateboard shop in Encinitas, California. *Lucia Daniella Griggi*

Lannnnnnnnnnnce Mounnnnntennnnnn! Tommyyyyyyyyyyyyyy Guerreroooooooooooo! Annnnnnnnnnnnnnnnd, Miiiiiiiiiike MuhGillllllllllllll!" And when Mike dropped in the crowd immediately started chanting: 'MACK-TWEEST! MACK-TWEEST! MACK-TWEEST!'

"Had there been a roof . . . !

"McGill managed to stretch it out for his first run... then, on his second run he busted a few airs and then launched into his signature move, pulled it, and blasted to the other wall, another McTwist! And then another! And then to the roll-out with his arms raised! You know those moments in sports when the angel of silence blesses the millisecond of recognition. The 'Holy-Crap-Did-You-Just-See-That-Moment?' Those kids went nuts. Tommy turned to me, 'So, I'll be leaving the ramp now. I think I'll see if one of those bikinis knows where we can get a cold beer?' That was a good good night. Mike ruled. The Bones Brigade ruled. We were on fire! In fact, there were flame machines, too. Epic. Let's do it again."

CHAPTER 7

Tony Hawk takes off into the stratosphere in the skateboard big air competition during the ESPN X-Games on August 5, 2004, at the Staples Center in Los Angeles, California. *Harry How/Getty Images*

Perhaps becoming more aware of skateboarding's profit-oriented side, and like all youth becoming increasingly aware of their own general colonization by business interests, skateboarders have also tried to resist the commodification of skateboarding by, curiously, returning to mainstream products and rejecting skateboarding-targeted products. The logic here is a complex one, and is predicated once again on the need for a subcultural identity to remain apart from more normative lifestyles. Skateboarding has always had its own clothes and safety equipment associated with it, including, in the 1970s and 1980s, specialist shoes from manufacturers such as Vans (founded 1966) and Vision, protective pads from Rector, helmets from Protec and Norton, plus a vast range of proprietary socks, shorts, t-shirts, and caps which constituted skateboarding style.

In the late 1980s and 1990s, however, skateboarding became a more fashionable activity in general, skateboard clothing became extremely popular in mainstream culture. For example, in 1997 specialist skateboard shoes by firms such as Vans, Airwalk, Converse, and DC could be found in mass-market stores. . . . Vans and Airwalk reached an annual turnover of $100 and $200 million respectively by 1996. Vans in particular successfully made the transition into global non-skate markets, becoming by the year 2000 a NASDAQ-traded company, with extensive overseas (non-U.S.) manufacturing operations. Clothes such as those by Stussy, originally marketed to skateboarders

That lady skates like a dude! The XX chromosome answer to X Games star Andy Macdonald and crossover skater/snowboarder Shaun White, Cara-Beth Burnside learned to skateboard at twelve, went to UC Davis on a soccer scholarship, collected aluminum cans to pay for snowboarding lift tickets . . . and went on to win gold medals at the X Games in skateboarding, and also competed at the Nagano, Japan, Olympics in snowboarding. *Lucia Daniella Griggi*

Bob Burnquist gets primed for the Skateboard Big Air Rail Jam Final during the Summer X Games XVI on July 31, 2010 in Los Angeles, California. *Bo Bridges/Getty Images*

Bob Burnquist uses the Force—aka centripetal acceleration—to complete the Loop of Death. *J. Grant Brittain*

in the 1980s, similarly became general high-street fare. As a result, suspicious of the reappropriation of a skate-style by non-skaters, some skateboarders have given up wearing their own subcultural clothing. In doing so, skaters implicitly realize that the right to be different is meaningful only when based on actions to establish differences, and thus that their identity is based on the activity of skateboarding, and not purely on the style adopted in clothes, shoes, and so forth.

In other words, a lot of core skateboard companies started getting rich by selling skate style to civilians—non-skaters who wanted to just walk in Airwalks, but not scuff them by grinding rails or knee-sliding down the sides of ramps or pools. That didn't sell well with a lot of core skaters, so skate fashion went spinning off in other directions that looked nothing like what the companies were selling to the proles.

So really, it was five major influences that helped skateboarding evolve in the 1990s: the Rocco Revolution, the X Games, the shoes/soft goods boom, the internet, and that obscure California law that officially labeled sidewalk surfing as something that the California Medical Association labeled it in 1965: a hazardous recreational activity.

Tony Hawk breaks the law—of gravity.
J. Grant Brittain

THE 900

Arguably the biggest moment in X Games skateboard history came at the turn of the century, during X Games V in San Francisco, when Tony Hawk pulled off the first 900—two and a half rotations—on the X Games ramp.

On June 27, 1999, at San Francisco's Pier 30, Tony Hawk was one of several vert skaters—including Andy Macdonald, Bucky Lasek, and Bob Burnquist—competing in the twenty-minute Best Trick competition.

Hawk landed a 720 varial on his first run during regulation time, and then he began going for the 900, as the announcers picked up on the attempt and began to incite the crowd.

Hawk talked about the move in a 2004 interview with David Kohn for *CBS News*: "I thought about it for nine years prior to that, but I never had the guts to spin it, and every once in a while I'd try to land one. I fractured a rib. And I threw my back out. And just came up short. Whatever could go wrong went wrong. I hit my shins on the top of the ramp. And I started to think maybe it's just not possible, you know? And I didn't really know. And so along came the X Games."

Hawk ate it, and ate it again and again, and failed four times before regulation time ran out. But Hawk kept going; the crowd was amped to see history made, and Tony was amped to make it: "This is the X Games! We make up our own rules!" the announcer said.

Hawk's face was covered with sweat and a look of absolute determination—the determination that had driven him his whole life. On his eleventh attempt, Hawk twirled his lanky, 6'3", 31-year-old frame through the air. He landed in a flat squat, his hand brushed the bottom of the vert ramp, but he recovered, did a turn on the other side of the ramp, and then claimed it.

Hawk was mobbed on the bottom of the ramp by friends and competitors, like a pitcher who had just thrown a perfect game. The face that had been twisted with sweat and determination was now smiling.

The move cemented the Tony Hawk legend and etched it in gold. The guy who'd been put on a five-dollar-a-day Taco Bell allowance at the beginning of the 1990s—and lost one of his homes and his wife to hard times—shot back into the stratosphere, in part because of the nationwide and international publicity he got from pulling off the impossible at the X Games.

Hawk summed up the moment later to Charlie Rose: "I just felt this great sense of relief that I'd finally conquered this beast that had plagued me for so long. And after that, it was just crazy. I mean it was like they put a highlight on *SportsCenter*. People would call me. I was incessantly interviewing about the 900. . . . And all of a sudden, everyone knows."

Hawk finished third out of five in Best Trick, because he made the 900 after regulation time had run out. But he made history that day, and the 900 in June 1999 was the capper to an extravagant decade in skateboarding—a 9.00 on the Richter scale in terms of who soared, who disappeared, who came back, and who prospered.

Six months later, the world was supposed to come to an end because of the Y2K bug, but it didn't, and Hawk's 900 seemed to launch skateboarding into the twenty-first century, as everyone strived to go big and follow the example Hawk had set. Skateboarding went up and out of the 1990s like Charlie in the Great Glass Elevator.

And it's still going.

Rodney Mullen began adapting his freestyle moves to street in the 1980s and into the 1990s. It was a big deal—the skate equivalent of Bob Dylan in 1965, walking onstage at the Newport Folk Festival with an electric guitar, backed by an electric band. Mullen electrified street skating in the 1980s, and brought a cornucopia of moves that helped street skating usurp vert into the 1990s. This is Mullen, airwalking through the streets of San Francisco.
J. Grant Brittain

Danny Way—a durable symbol for the bigness
of twenty-first century skateboarding, and
also the toughness, ambition, and dedication.
Lucia Daniella Griggi

ANYTHING GOES BIG

CHAPTER 8

IT'S ALL FINE AND DANDY HERE IN THE FIRST DECADE OF THE 21st CENTURY

Clearly the world didn't come grinding to a halt when the clock struck midnight for Y2K. And strangely, neither did skateboarding. Ten years after vert was being outranked by street skating, and Stacy Peralta left Powell-Peralta, and Tony Hawk had a Taco Bell budget—skateboarding was moving into the new millenium higher, faster, and bigger. From Wall Street to the Great Wall of China.

Skateboarding went big in the twenty-first century—big in terms of core and civilian media coverage, big in terms of mega ramps, and big in terms of money. Very big. The part of skateboarding that hates the whole corporate, merchandising, branding, marketing side of the business isn't going to like this, but the reason skateboarding didn't crash in the transition from street

The Great Wall of China setup, enough to make even Genghis Khan tap his saber on the coping in salute. The 65-foot-high ramp propelled Danny Way at around 55 mph and launched him over the 70-foot width of the wall. Once clear, he landed on a 100-foot-long ramp before soaring again off a 30-foot-tall quarterpipe. *Getty Images*

ANYTHING GOES BIG

235

SHOOTER

J. GRANT BRITTAIN SHOOTS SKATEBOARDERS

J. Grant Brittain has been shooting skateboarding going all the way back to the days of film.

Condensing Miki Vuckovich's biography of Brittain from his website: Brittain began shooting his friends in 1979 when he worked at the Del Mar Skate Ranch, when cameras were measured in millimeters, not megapixels. He took classes at Palomar Junior College to get his tech skills down, and in 1983 he contributed his photos to the premiere issue of *TransWorld Skateboarding Magazine*. That lead to Brittain taking the position of photo editor and senior photographer, and that gave him access to heaps of 35mm film. He's been shooting ever since, making the transition from film to digital cameras, shooting every relevant skateboarder from the 1980s and well into the twenty-first century.

"Few photographers have pursued so wide a range of subjects and styles," Vuckovich wrote. "But few individuals find themselves so central to such an active community, where one's perspective is just a notch askew of the rest, and where movement and progression is the norm."

After *TWS* was bought by larger corporate interests, Brittain and his cadre left that magazine to start their own: *The Skateboard Mag*. The photography in that magazine is excellent.

Up close and personal with J. Grant Brittain and a device they used to call a "film camera." *Lucia Daniella Griggi*

DENNIS MARTINEZ DOES A 360

Why do they call it DOPE? Because it leads to Death or Prison Eventually. According to Mar Yvette in *Dispatch Magazine*, Dennis Martinez was a skate star of the 1970s, sponsored by Bahne, G&S, Alva, and others. Martinez turned pro in 1977 and won the World Cup Skateboarding Championship in 1978.

Martinez was only sixteen when he was ruling the skateboard world, and he quickly figured out that the guys who were making the covers of skateboard magazines were the guys giving drugs to the photographers and editors: "Little did Martinez know that his method of getting on the covers of magazines was about to lead him on a twenty-year path of addiction and destruction," Yvette writes.

Martinez began using cocaine to boost his performance in skate competitions. Cocaine use turned to heroin, and by the 1980s, Martinez was selling his 1970s trophies to buy more dope. He overdosed twice, and later, deciding he didn't want to die or go to prison, began a life of sobriety in 1996.

Ten years later, Martinez was a married man with children and a pastor working at Training Center, a drug and alcohol treatment center for men.

Dennis Martinez. *Lucia Daniella Griggi*

Skatepark designer Zach Wormhoudt, pondering what further cement sickness he can unleash on the skateboard world. This portrait was taken at the Ken Wormhoudt Skate Park, next to the San Lorenzo River in the Wormhoudts' hometown of Santa Cruz. The park is named for his father, who was involved in the design of dozens of California's skateparks. As of 2010, Wormhoudt Inc. (run by Zach and his brother Jake) has designed more than 125 skate- and bikeparks around the world and consulted with more than 450 communities on making facilities that were rad, safe, and cutting edge. *Lucia Daniella Griggi*

"Hey! No photos!" is kind of a weird pose for Steve Sherman to take, as he has been taking quality snaps going all the way back to the 1970s. A prolific surf and skate shooter, Sherman got launched on his arc by exposure to the La Costa scene in the early days: "La Costa was like the North Shore of skateboarding at this time. Big hills, massive speed, and state of the art slalom courses . . . As a kid in Poway I was in awe that the place even existed." *Lucia Daniella Griggi*

Why is this man laughing? This is Johnny Schillereff, the founder and president of Element Skateboards, and he's laughing because he does what he loves. But this life of skateboarding and smiles didn't come easy. Over two decades of instability and disbelief, Johnny's hard work persevered, and made Element what it is today: the leading skateboard company of the twenty-first century. *Lucia Daniella Griggi*

GOING MEGA

ow it's 2010—a little over ten years since Hawk spun his 900. Whether or not that move was the landmark for the next ten-year skateboarding cycle, a perusal of the current skateboarding scene shows that it's more than a little healthy.

In May 2010, George Powell addressed the IASC Skateboarding Industry Summit, addressing the growing threat from outsiders: "If all we as an industry choose to think about is maximizing our own profit, gaining market share, or stealing somebody else's team rider, instead of banding together in a cohesive voice, then the powerful entities helping themselves to skateboarding will simply walk away with a very special sport, the culture, and the industry we created during the three decades of hard work and dedication to the preservation of skateboarding as a free and evolving activity."

The skateboard industry in 2010 is worth billions: wheels, trucks, decks, graphics, shoes, socks, ankle protection, shin protection, kneepads, skateboard shorts, hip and butt pads, belts, gloves, t-shirts, skate jewelry, skate tattoos, skate glasses, safety helmets. America has three major skateboarding magazines and dozens of zines— *Thrasher* is preparing to celebrate its thirtieth anniversary by putting every issue of the magazine online.

TransWorld Skateboarding was sold to Times Mirror in 1999, and became a part of AOL Time Warner in 2000. *Skateboard* magazine spun off from *TransWorld* in 2004, when J. Grant Brittain, Dave Swift, and Atiba Jefferson decided they didn't like being under the mantle of AOL Time Warner, and walked out to form their own magazine.

Then there is www.skateboardingmagazine.com, and hundreds of other print and online skate zines: *Skatedork, Skate and Annoy, SauceSkateBoardZine, BoredZine, PayingPain, Juice Magazine, Dan's Zine, Expose Magazine, SkateRock.com, Brotherhood, Heyday Skateboarding, Influx Magazine, Negativeion, Skateboarding Sux,* and many others around the world.

The website at www.theskateboardindustry.com published "A Detailed Analysis of Board Company Sales Over Six Years," by Rob Meronek, who explained the list:

This listing shows the top selling board companies over the last six years and their percentage changes in sales each year. The data is from the Skatepark of Tampa point of sale system that I wrote back in 2001. . . . Only board companies that sold at least one hundred decks in this time are included. The data only includes boards sold in the Shop, not on the website: Baker, Zero, Flip, Element, Zoo York, DGK, Girl, Habitat, Alien Workshop, Anti-Hero, Black Label, Mystery, Krooked, Chocolate, Foundation, Real, Almost, Toy Machine, Plan B, enjoi, Blind, Powell, Popwar, Darkstar, Expedition One, Consolidated, Organika, Lib Tech, Birdhouse, Stereo, World Industries, Rasa Libre, Listen Skateboards, 151 Skateboards, Shorty's, Santa Cruz, Aesthetics.

And those are just the deck companies that sold over a hundred boards in the shop, not online. There are scores of other deck companies. Some of them come and go like fireflies, and some of them have been around since the 1970s.

The first decade of the twenty-first century was all about going mega, and that's exactly what the skateboard industry has done. By 2010, the Leisure Trends Group reported the core skate retail industry was about $2.41 billion.

A billion here and a billion there, and pretty soon you're talking real money.

As the song goes, "He doesn't look a thing like Jesus, but he talks like a gentleman." Brian "Slash" Hansen is something like that, one of the faces of twenty-first Century West Coast street skating. Possessor of a full bag of skate tricks and known for doing to the streets of Los Angeles what Gonz does to the streets of New York and Bart Simpson does to the streets of Springfield.
Lucia Daniella Griggi